Work Smarter: Live Better

Work Smarter: Live Better

PRACTICAL WAYS TO CHANGE YOUR WORK HABITS AND TRANSFORM YOUR LIFE

Cyril Peupion

Work Smarter: Live Better
Published by Peupion Pty Ltd atf Peupion Family Trust
1 Sheaffe Place, Davidson NSW 2085, Australia
www.wslb.com.au

First published 2010 (reprinted 5 times). Edited 2014.
Limited edition for kikki.K first published 2014 (ISBN 9332403060192)

© 2010, 2014 Peupion Pty Ltd
The moral rights of the author have been asserted.

National Library of Australia
Cataloguing-in-Publication data

Author	Peupion, Cyril.
Title	*Work Smarter: Live Better* / Cyril Peupion.
ISBN	9780646544502 (pbk.)
Subjects	Quality of work life. Work-life balance.

Dewey Number 306.361

Work Smarter: Live Better is an independent publication and has not been authorised, sponsored or otherwise approved by any corporation or person referred in this publication or by the owners of any trade mark referred to in this publication.

iPhone®, iPad™ and iPod® are registered trademarks of Apple Inc., registered in the US and other countries.

Microsoft Excel®, Microsoft Outlook 2007®, Microsoft Outlook 2010®, Microsoft PowerPoint® and Microsoft Word® are either registered trademarks or trademarks of Microsoft Corporation in the United States and/or other countries.

Lotus® is a registered trademark of IBM®.

Every effort has been made to ensure that sources for work quoted in this material are noted accurately. Please contact the publisher with any details that should be included in reprinted editions.

Editor	Jo McKee	www.editonline.com.au
Design	Graham Rendoth	www.renodesign.com.au
Photographs	istockphoto.com (cover, page xii), dreamstime.com (page 186)
Printing	Toppan Security Printing

Dedication

To my love, support and confidante, TK, my wonderful wife without whom life would not be as rich and spontaneous.

To my three amazing kids: Fleur, Cameron and Mirabelle, who make me want to live each day with them as fully as if it were the last, and make my life with them last forever.

PRAISE FOR CYRIL PEUPION AND HIS JOURNEY TO CHALLENGE WORK HABITS

'I remember the first time I put an appointment in my diary to drop my daughter at school. It felt rather strange, as though I wasn't making most use of my time. I soon realised it's quite the opposite. I'm now managing my time to make sure I do the things that matter.'

Stuart Hall
General Manager, Retail Centre of Excellence
St George Bank

'The search for optimum efficiency became one big step closer thanks to Cyril's very real, concrete but also progressive recommendations and lessons. Four years after I took the course, those lessons have become an integral part of not only who I am as a Manager, but who I am as a person.

'There are not many courses that one takes and keeps as daily carry-on luggage: lessons that make a real difference, lessons that allowed me to be more productive even with the most simple tasks.'

Jerome Casteigt
General Manager Nespresso Australia
Nestlé

'It is easy to major on the minors, striving for effectiveness but getting distracted on the little things. Cyril helped me develop the "efficiency habit", giving me more time to be effective at what really matters. ... Doing things right gives me more time on the right things.'

Peter Nicholas
Director, Customer Value
AMP Financial Services

"I estimate we saved between half a million dollars to a million dollars of cost thanks to this journey. As importantly, the increased focus of the team probably accelerated some key projects by about six months. It is hard to quantify the impact on our revenue and performance, but I know it is huge.'

Neil Younger
Head of Dealer Group
BT Financial Group

'Your approach is sensational! It is extremely practical and challenging, but realistic in its attempts to change behaviours. I saw real results immediately, for myself and my team.

'I am now more focused on doing more of the right things. I spend more time, about two hours more per day, on the things that matter and disregard the things that don't. I spend more time with clients and developing key relationships as opposed to mundane administrative and email tasks that were all-consuming.

'This program has created lasting positive changes on the way I work.'

Giles Gunesekera
Director, Head of Third Party Sales
Principal Global Investors

'The journey with Cyril delivered an immediate and lasting impact on the sense of purpose of all team members. Clarity of focus on the activities which count has improved group achievement as well as the way team members inter-work with others. Beyond this, improved ways of working have resulted in less intrusion of work into my personal time.'

Philip Park
General Manager National Planning & Development
NSW | SingTel Optus

'The main impact is that I sleep at night. I didn't realise the impact of my work on my stress levels. I was working long hours and coming home stressed. Since working with Cyril, I am far less stressed. I sleep at night. He changed my life!'

Marnie McLaren
Head of Investment Sourcing
St George Wealth Management

'I couldn't run my business as effectively and profitably as I do had I not learnt these efficiency and effectiveness skills.

'I am far more productive than I was, and get SO much more of the important stuff done. Plus, I now use my brain for thinking, strategising and processing important information, not trying to remember what I have to do, so I rarely miss anything and I'm far less stressed, both at work and at home. ... I recommend everyone learns and applies these skills!'

Simon Smith
Managing Director
Southern Cross Coaching & Development Pty Ltd

'While I thought I was a good planner and had balance in my day-to-day work, I have actually dramatically changed the way I manage my time and also priorities. Most rewarding is the personal time I have built into my working week that ensures I spend quality time with my family.

'I have not had to sacrifice my work commitments, but instead have created time to think about what is strategically most important. ... Hopefully this feedback does justice to the full impact Cyril has had upon me.'

Stuart Blake
Head of Sales & Service
NRMA, SGIO & SGIC – IAG

Acknowledgements

To Bettina Pidcock, my first client, who pushed me to write this book and helped me along this journey.

To the St George Bank team: Jason, Neil, Geoff, Marnie, Matt and so many others. You gave me so much in your feedback and support.

To some great people who have helped me to publish this book: my editor Jo McKee, and my designer Graham Rendoth, who did a terrific job in a challenging time frame. The two of you have been amazing in helping me in this journey.

Contents

Overview

SO YOU THINK YOU CAN WORK?

Most of us have never been taught how to work.

A very bold statement to start with …

However this is one of the most important reasons for lack of execution and lower-than-expected performance. Most of us are committed to our role and want to do a good job. We are neither lazy nor unwilling. But we are not always working efficiently; we are working hard but not always smart.

Quite often we believe that to increase our performance, our revenue or our profits, we need to do more. We believe we must work longer hours, make more phone calls and attend more meetings. And in our busy working life, doing more is either almost impossible or carries a high price. We spend less time with our loved ones, we neglect our health, we put some of our passions and hobbies on the back burner and we end up frustrated, feeling out of control and stressed.

Disorganised work environments, unread emails, missed deadlines and feeling overwhelmed and stressed are real pressures for many people in their working days. Most of us spend important parts of our day on low-value activities, failing to deliver high performance. This greatly impacts on our ability to perform, on the performance of our people and on the performance of our company.

This book is not about having a tidy desk and a clean inbox. It is much more than that.

Cyril Peupion's main focus is to improve companies' performances and change people's lives by challenging their work habits. Cyril will challenge your way of thinking about performance and give you simple and practical tools to be more effective, to focus on the right things. You will learn how to become a proactive leader rather than just being a reactive follower.

Introduction

An evening in Paris

It was a comfortable Paris evening. We had enjoyed dinner and were about to go out to watch a movie. I was with my closest friends. I was happy. I was feeling great. Then someone asked, 'Have you heard about Sophie? Her father has been diagnosed with cancer and only has a few weeks to live.'

Sophie's father had not yet retired. He had worked hard all his life, and was just about to enjoy a well-deserved and wealthy retirement. He had a lovely family and was looking forward to spending more time with his wife, children and soon grandchildren.

But now this would never happen.

Later, it hit me more than I had realised at the time. Gradually, the questions took hold and grew within me. Is this what life is about? Working long hours most of your life to retire too old and too tired to really enjoy the things you always wanted to do and the people you really love? Or worse, dying before that retirement can even begin?

It made me realise the value of time and enjoyment of life day after day, to take every day as potentially the last. In all fairness it took many years for me to absorb the lesson of that evening. And I am sure I am continuing to digest it.

When delivering the commencement speech to Stanford University students in 2005, Steve Jobs, CEO of Apple Inc, made this interesting statement:

> *'For the past 33 years, I have looked in the mirror every morning and asked myself: "If today was the last day of my life, would I want to do what I am about to do today?"*

'And whenever the answer has been "No" for too many days in a row, I know I need to change something ... almost everything.

'All external expectations, all pride, all fear of embarrassment or failure — these things just fall away in the face of death, leaving only what is truly important.'

Although the intention of this book is to get your business life back in control, focusing on what is truly important for you is really what this book is about. Do you live your life, both personally and professionally, as if each day were potentially the last? Do you wake up every day feeling 100% positive about the day?

When is your day?

I would like you to imagine something crazy. Imagine you have just won the lottery. You won five million dollars, and the money has just been transferred to your bank account. The dream is now a reality, the money is yours. What would you do with this money? Be honest, crazy, fun. What would you buy with it, small and big, long term and short term?

When I ask this question in my seminars, I get both serious long-term answers as well as fun short-term crazy spending ideas: 'I'll pay off my mortgage,'; 'I'll invest in real estate,'; 'I'll invest in shares,' ... as well as, 'I'll buy a nice convertible,'; 'I'll go travelling for a year,'; 'I'll buy my wife and kids some amazing presents.' One woman even said she would go on a shoe shopping frenzy ...

Imagine now you won the lottery, but the prize comes with strings attached to it. You have won five million dollars, but you cannot earn, win or inherit any more money for the rest of your life. You can invest some or all of the five million. However, even if you work, you can't earn a salary. All you have to play with is this five million dollars. What would you do with this money?

When I ask this second question, most of the fun or short-term answers suddenly evaporate. Most people are now thinking about paying off their debts and investing, seeking some financial advice and planning carefully how to manage their money.

Interestingly enough, when the amount of something is limited we better appreciate the value of it. We put more effort into thinking about it and planning what to do with it.

Third test. You must be thinking by now that this is a very strange lottery indeed. And you are right. Imagine this time the lottery man comes with a different proposition. He is holding a briefcase with some money inside. You don't know how much money is inside the briefcase. There could be anything between five dollars and a hundred million dollars. There could be $5, $10, $100, $1000, $1 million ... you do not know.

However this time the offer is different: it's a 'deal or no deal'. If you take the briefcase, and the money within, we will take all your belongings and the money in the briefcase is all you will have for the rest of your life. You cannot earn, win or inherit any more money for the rest of your life. You can invest some or all of the money. However, even if you work, you can't earn a salary. All you have to play with is the amount in the briefcase.

You could be lucky and end up with a hundred million dollars, or be unlucky and end up with only five dollars for the rest of your life. Deal or no deal? Would you take the briefcase?

I have had a few people who have been tempted — less than 1%. The overwhelming majority of people would not take this deal.

Fourth and last test. Same proposition as the third test. The lottery man comes with a briefcase with some money inside, anything from five dollars to a hundred million dollars. Same as the previous proposition: if you take the briefcase, all your belongings will be taken away from you and all you will have to invest is the money inside the case.

The difference with the previous proposition is that there is a small opening on the briefcase with a $5 note sticking out. The briefcase is built so that whenever you take the $5 note, another one appears. You cannot open the briefcase; you have to take the money note by note.

The big difference with the previous deal is that even if you take the deal you won't know how much money there is in the briefcase. You will have to take the money, one $5 note after another, until it stops. And of course you don't know if there is only one $5 note, and the money will stop after the first withdrawal, or if there is a hundred million dollars; i.e. an almost endless flow of $5 notes.

Would you take the deal?

So far I haven't found anyone interested.

Yet, if you substitute money for time, this is the deal we are given. We live a minute and another minute appears. We live another minute and another one appears. No-one knows how many minutes we have in our briefcase. We could be gone in a day, in a week, in a year, in ten years. Who knows?

We are given a terrible deal with time — a deal no one would accept with money. However we place much more value on our money than on our time.

Imagine someone steals your wallet while you're walking in the street. There might only be a few dollars in it, or a few notes, but you would try to do something about it. Run behind the thief if you can, shout, try to arrest him and prosecute him. You would be very upset.

Every day we allow our time to be stolen and we do not react. Time is far more important than money, and we place so little value on it.

Imagine that someone comes to you and asks for $100. You would ask why and would need some good reasons to give $100 away. However, when someone invites us for a meeting or interrupts us, asking for our time, we are far less careful. We give our time away very easily.

I don't know how long you and I will be here. What I do know is that I want to make every day, every hour, every minute count as if it were gold.

In this book I have included some of the principles by which I live. I share these with my clients to make sure they are as effective as possible, helping them achieve what is important for them.

Some interesting facts about how we work

I am always surprised, and even amazed, to see how much time we waste every day on things that really do not matter. The problem is not the fact that we are spending time on non-important matters; it's the consequences of this. It's the fact that we are not spending enough time on things which are very important to us, such as family, health, the key projects at work which will have a big impact on our performance, and so on.

In recent years, the advances in technology at work have been phenomenal. We now have amazing tools at our fingertips which are available to everyone. If you think of email, research by the Lotus Development Corporation shows that people are receiving on average forty to fifty emails per day. Some of my clients are getting over 200 emails every day.

This is great on one view. A high level of communications ought to signify a high level of productivity in our businesses. But we are paying a high price for this. A few years ago one of my coachees heard a very interesting survey on the radio. Apparently in Australia white collar workers check their email, on average, 50 times per day ...

I cannot verify this survey but I know that people are constantly looking at their inbox. We start working on something, and we stop every few seconds to check whether we have received new emails. We continue concentrating on our work, and we hear the 'bing' from our inbox to indicate a new email has arrived. It's hard to resist — we humans are curious by nature — and here we are checking our emails again. We return to our work, and after ten minutes feel a bit bored. Guess what? We re-re-recheck our inbox!

Sound familiar? But it does not stop there. The recent move for many companies from compartmentalised offices to open plan workspaces adds to our lack of concentration. Research shows that, on average, people are interrupted every three minutes.

Although the above examples are mainly relevant to corporate life, they have an equally important impact upon our personal lives.

I have seen another survey which demonstrated that 66% of corporate strategy is never executed. Companies spend a lot of time and money to think ahead, to decide their long-term vision and strategy. They pay high-level consultants or recruit high fliers to do so. They involve many people and resources to produce a lovely Word document and numerous PowerPoint® slides to display their plan and strategy.

Only to see that two-thirds of it will never be executed.

In my experience, one of the biggest challenges for companies today is execution. They might be clear on their strategy, on where they want to head. But if you check what people are doing on a day-to-day basis, what they spend their time on hour per hour, you realise there is often a big gap between what they are doing and what they are supposed to do. There is a big gap between what they should be doing to have a major impact on the business, and what they are really doing.

Many people tell me one of their biggest frustrations is that they find themselves at the end of each day having worked hard on a lot of small crises, but having not had the time to focus on any of their big-ticket items.

The impact of our lack of efficiency and effectiveness does not stop in the workplace. When I ask my clients what they would like to do if they were more in control of their work and time, I often receive such answers as:

- 'Come home earlier to see my kids.'
- 'Have more time to go to the gym and look after my health.'
- 'Avoid bringing my work stress home.'
- 'Avoid waking up at night thinking about what I forgot to do.'

Inefficiency impacts us both at work and at home.

Most of us have never been taught how to work

What a bold statement to start with! However, in my view, this is one of the most important reasons for lack of execution and lower-than-expected performance. Most people are committed to their role and want to do a good job. They are neither lazy nor unwilling. But they are not working efficiently — they work hard but not always smart. They have never been taught how to work.

It normally surprises people when I make this claim, but I believe most people have never been taught how to work. We go to school, universities, and gain a qualification. We train and qualify as doctors, accountants or engineers. And one day we start working.

Let's take some simple examples. We get a desk and a computer, and before we know it we get bombarded with information. We receive many emails and have to handle many paper documents.

In my career as an effectiveness coach I have seen many 'information management systems'. From people who have nothing on their desk, to people who have a few piles to remind them of the things to do for the day, to people who have huge reading piles, to people who have a desk which looks like a bombsite.

I have even met a few people who had two desks: the current one and the old one. They used to work on the old one, but it became so full of paper and files that they had to move to a new desk. And they still use their old desk as a filing system. Curious filing system indeed!

To have a laugh with some of my clients I sometime take pictures of their desk before I begin working with them. One day I might ask my clients if I can publish some of these pictures — you would not believe your eyes!

When I ask people why they chose this 'information management system', the most common answer is, 'Trial and error.' I then ask if this is the best system for them, and I hear, 'I don't know — I have never been shown how to do this.'

Another example which demonstrates that most of us have never been taught how to work is the way we manage our priorities. The most common way I have observed is what I call the 'note pad strategy'. At the start of every day, you start a new 'to do' list in your note pad. You write all the tasks which need to be done for the day.

On one hand people enjoy having a 'to do list'. They can keep track of everything they have to do and they can add things throughout the day.

On the other hand they are often frustrated with this system. New things keep being added to their list. They finish the day with half of the list not completed. And at the start of a new day they have to scramble through all their previous 'to do' lists to collect all undone or unfinished items.

When I ask people why they do it this way, I get answers such as, 'I have so many things to do every day that I need a system to keep track of all this.' When asked if this is the most effective system for them, most people don't know. They have never been taught some simple yet effective work habits.

As most people have never been shown how to work, they have developed work habits that are not the most efficient and effective ones. There is nothing wrong or shameful in this. Peter Drucker was one of the most famous effectiveness coaches. He wrote many books including the famous *The Effective Executive*. In this book he wrote:

> *'In forty-five years of work as a consultant I have not come across a single natural, an executive who was born effective. All the effective ones have had to learn to be effective. And all of them had to practise effectiveness until it became a habit.'*

We are not born naturally effective. We have to learn the principles and practise them until they become habits.

My main focus is to improve the performance of individuals, teams or divisions by challenging their work habits. And the lift in productivity and performance by simply improving people's work habits is amazing. So much time, energy and money is wasted because of poor execution.

The purpose of this book

The purpose of this book could be viewed solely as a guide to improving your performance at work by giving you simple and practical tools to be more effective.

While I want to help you to improve your productivity by challenging your work habits, my ambition in writing this book is to have an impact not only on your business life but also your personal one. Business and personal life are intrinsically linked. If you are out of control and stressed at work, it will affect your personal life.

As an effectiveness coach, my personal motivation comes from hearing the impact I've had on the lives of my coachees. My ambition is to change the life of each person I interact with. It may sound ambitious, but this is what drives me. Comments such as, 'You have changed my life,' or 'I feel so much more in control and happy with my job,' or 'My performance has dramatically increased since I have worked with you,' are my best rewards.

I will never forget the first person who gave me this feedback. It was the last session with one of our first clients, a group of managers from a bank. I was asking each participant for their feedback, for the changes they had made throughout the four months' journey we had undertaken, and the impact of those changes.

The feedback from the team was terrific. The journey had had an amazing impact on their work habits and they were all very positive about it. And then Marnie stood up and explained the impact for her. She mentioned that as a result of this journey, she felt much more organised, her desk was cleaner, she was on top of her emails, she was much more focused. As a result she had no doubt she would over-achieve her KPIs (key performance indicators), and that she would achieve her business goals for this year.

And then Marnie made an amazing comment. She said that this was not the big win for her; that this was not the most important thing. I was intrigued. What Marnie had mentioned so far sounded great and I was pleased she had achieved so much throughout the program.

Marnie said something I will never forget: 'The big win for me is that I sleep at night.' I was not expecting this and asked Marnie what she meant. She then explained, 'I have a challenging job. I love it, but for many years I have brought my stress home. I have found myself waking up in the middle of the night with ideas of things I should do or should have done, of things I had forgotten or let slip. I had to sleep with a note pad on my bedside table to write all this down.

'For the first time for many years, I sleep well at night. When I leave the office, I feel in control, I feel I have achieved what I need to. Even my husband is seeing the difference. This journey has changed my life.'

I was nearly in tears. This was one of those moments when you realise why you are doing what you are doing. This became the focus and vision for me, something that drives me forward — 'changing lives'. Since then 'changing lives' has become the mission of my business, Work Smarter: Live Better. A very ambitious mission, indeed. But if you do not aim high, you are unlikely to achieve great things or to bring great value.

I hope this book will help you to be more effective, to perform better at work and feel more in control of both your professional and personal life. Ultimately my goal and hope is that this book changes your life.

Efficiency versus effectiveness

When I mention in the corporate world that the focus of my business is to increase performance by challenging people's work habits, I am often met with doubt.

Performance is a well-worn word, used in all industries and for whatever is being sold. What a company does or purchases is ultimately aimed at improving its bottom line and performance. Performance means so many different things that I sometimes feel the word has lost its power because of misuse and over-use.

When we deal with a sales team, performance is usually quite easy to define. It can be measured, for example, by the number of meetings or the amount of revenue and profit. When we deal with a legal team, performance is more difficult to measure. In some law firms it is measured in billable hours per day. Other legal teams link performance to internal feedback and satisfaction. Or a combination of both.

When we work with a marketing team or a senior executive, performance has yet another meaning. In this case performance can be linked to the revenue generated from marketing activities, to indicators such as improved brand recognition or client satisfaction, or to the delivery of specific projects.

However there are often two criteria that influence performance. Let's take a few examples. When you discuss *performance* with a sales team, you will hear success measured using these factors:

■ **Performance (sales) = quantity x quality**

On one hand you can be a great sales person, have a very good understanding of your products, target the right clients, and have a very good sales approach (quality). However, if you do not make any phone calls and have no meetings (quantity), it will be hard to perform.

On the other hand you can be a dynamic sales person, make lots of phone calls and have lots of meetings (quantity); if you do not target the right prospects, if you do not know your products well and have poor sales skills (quality), it will be hard to perform.

When we think about *people management*, we often hear about two different skills: management skills and leadership skills.

■ **Performance (leading team) = management x leadership**

You can be a great manager, have clearly defined KPIs for your team, have organised regular one-on-ones, team meetings and reviews, and you spend lots of time with your team; but if you are leading them in the wrong direction, if you do not have the right vision and strategy, it will be very hard for you and your team to perform.

You can have a great vision for your team and have clear strategies in your head to make your team successful but if you do not communicate with them, if they are unclear on this vision, if you do not define clearly the role of each and monitor and coach them on a regular basis, it will also be hard to be successful.

In terms of *personal productivity*, there are two critical skills that impact personal performance: efficiency and effectiveness.

■ **Performance (personal) = efficiency x effectiveness**

Quantity, management and efficiency are all linked to 'how' you do things. When you are given a task or a project, how well do you do it? Do you carry it out as requested, do you respect the budget, do you pay attention to detail, do you do it on time and respect deadlines? Efficiency can be defined by doing things right.

Quality, leadership and effectiveness are all linked to 'what' you are doing. Are you focusing on the few crucial things which will be key for your performance? Effectiveness can be defined by doing the right things.

To be more in control of your workload, to work smarter rather than harder, I will discuss these two skills: efficiency (doing things right, i.e. the 'how') and effectiveness (doing the right things, i.e. the 'what').

I will start with the 'how'. Are your work habits slowing your performance? Do you have an efficient filing system? Do you manage as efficiently as possible the flow of information and tasks you receive on a daily basis?

I will then discuss a great efficiency tool: Microsoft Outlook*. To be both efficient and effective, you need a tool to manage your time, your tasks, your focus. In the business world, most people are using Outlook, while some are using Lotus® Notes and a few are using other systems such as GroupWise, a device such as a smartphone, BlackBerry® or iPad™, or even a paper tool. The principles we will discuss are equally relevant for Outlook, Lotus® or whatever system you are using. Because most people use Outlook, I will use this tool as an example.

Then I will focus on effectiveness, what I call personal leadership. This is more the 'what'.

Although I start with efficiency principles, the most important principles are the effectiveness principles. For many years, time management books and seminars have been focusing on saving time, on doing things quickly. Saving time is important but is almost irrelevant if you are not clear on what you want to achieve, if you are not clear on what is important for you.

I'd rather be very effective and totally inefficient than the contrary. In business terms, I believe a person with a messy desk, emails out of control and bad time-wasting habits but who is clear on what he or she wants to achieve, and making some progress towards those goals, will be more successful than a person who is well organised, with a clean desk and an inbox under control, with great work habits but no goals, and who is unclear regarding the few things which are key for his or her performance.

Having said that, I have found it more beneficial over the years to start improving efficiency and then work on effectiveness principles. I found it works better to put the house in order and then discuss long-term goals and focus.

I have found that people are much more receptive to taking a 10,000 feet high helicopter view of their role and goals once they feel in control of their day-to-day activities. Hence my logic in starting with the efficiency principles before the effectiveness ones.

Reading is easy, changing habits is hard

At this point it would be useful for you to be clear on why you are reading this book and what are you expecting from it. Are you reading it for leisure or do you want to see some real changes? Do you want to challenge some of your work habits?

Being clear on your goals will give you the fuel and energy to act. If you want to be successful and achieve your dreams, the most important thing is not the 'how', it's the 'why'.

Throughout this book I would like to share some principles that are important to perform if you are to be successful. Rather than settle for just showing you, I would like to take you through a journey and challenge some of your work habits, some of those things you are doing every day and that you have probably been doing for many years. The principles are simple, but changing them into habits is hard.

If you do not have strong reasons to change, what I will suggest in this book will be very challenging, and you will struggle to find the motivation and drive to apply these principles.

- Let me ask you: Why are you reading this book? What are some of the challenges you are facing in the area of efficiency and effectiveness?

- Does your filing system need a good review?

- Are you crawling under a ton of emails in your inbox?

- Do you wonder every day what to focus on?

- Do you struggle to manage your time effectively?

- Are you frustrated at the end of every day, wondering where your time went?

- Do you have to take some important work at home or stay late in the evening when everyone else is gone so that you can finish it?

And beyond these challenges, what outcomes are you expecting? What do you want to change? What will be the business benefits and pay-offs of working more efficiently and effectively? Will you reach your targets, achieve your KPIs, be promoted to new responsibilities?

As importantly, what will be the personal benefits and pay-offs of working smarter? Will you spend fewer hours in the office and more time at home? Will you be less stressed? Will you feel more in control, able to enjoy your job again?

Reflect on this. Are you ready to take a journey which could transform your life? As mentioned earlier, my ambition whenever I coach someone is 'to change life.' I hope I can reach the same goal with everyone reading this book. To achieve this goal, I will need your help. If you want to be challenged and change some of your work habits, reading this book alone will not be enough. You will need to bring two things to the party: practice and persistence.

Practising is learning

Confucius is credited as saying: 'I hear and I forget, I see and I remember, I do and I understand.'

Reading this book alone is not enough. You need to read it carefully and you need to be ready to practise the principles explained. You need to read it as if you want to teach these principles to someone else.

Only then will you start to see some changes.

I suggest reading this book with a pen and a highlighter close by. Underline what resonates; what you want to remember. The action of underlining key phrases will fix them better in your mind and enable you to come back to the principles, materials and tools which resonated with you.

Once back at your desk, review the sections you have highlighted and the things you have decided to apply, *and just do it!*

Don't be a perfectionist. I used to be one, and nothing gets done because perfection is not achievable. Do not put off trying a new way of doing something just because now is not the perfect time. There will never be a perfect time. Try new skills as best as you can. Practise, persevere, and little by little you will improve.

I once read about some research done in the US by a psychiatrist who specialises in education, Doctor William Glasser. What he found out is very important in any learning process. Glasser demonstrated that we remember 10% of what we read, 20% of what we hear, 80% of what we practise and 95% of what we teach someone else.

If the only thing you do is read this book and that's it, you are likely to remember only 10% of it. In a one or two day training session where you hear a lot of good principles, you are likely to remember only 20% of it.

You can see the huge gap between only reading the material as opposed to hearing and practising the ideas. Your learning jumps from less than 20% to 80%. This is why simply reading a book or doing a training course often does not produce the results it should.

I heard once that on average we retain 12% to 15% of the learning from a simple training course. And this does not surprise me. However I find it amazing that we accept this from training. Imagine you buy a brand new car for $50,000 and on the day you are supposed to get it, you are given only four wheels — 10% of the value. No one would accept this. Why should we accept it from learning?

Whatever you find of value and relevance for you in this book, practise it back at your desk or in your workspace straight away.

If you want to see real change in your work habits, if you want to be more in control of your workloads, to work smarter and not harder, you need to read this book as if you were going to teach it to someone else and you need to practise the principles until they become new habits.

Persist to change the new learning into habits

My role will be to suggest some simple principles and challenge some of your work habits. Your role if you want to progress will be to do two things:

practise and persist. You understand the importance of practising. Let me explain why I mean by persisting.

There is a joke which says, 'Do you know the difference between a hassle and a habit? … two weeks.' For two weeks, doing something differently is a hassle. After two weeks of practice, it becomes a habit. There is a lot of truth in it. Changing some of your work habits will feel awkward to start with. You will be tempted to come back to your old work habits which are easier and more comfortable.

Just be aware of it. Changing your work habits will be hard for about two weeks. Studies on habits show it takes about twenty-one days to change a habit. If you are to persist every day with a new work principle, within twenty-one days it will have become a habit.

Be persistent. The rewards, which I see so often in the lives of those I coach, are clearly worth it.

Read, practise, persist and celebrate with me

My ambition is for you to take away something valuable from this book. I hope you will enjoy this book, learn a few things from it, apply those things and change some of your work habits.

Once you have made some progress, write to me and share what you have learnt and how you feel. Take a photo of your desk before and after practising new habits and send it to me. Let me know the number of emails in your inbox (read and unread) before and after. Share with me the impact these new habits have had on your performance, your stress level and your life.

I really enjoy receiving feedback. This is what drives me, hearing that our approach and methodology have made a difference. You may also have some ideas and tips you would like to share. Please do not hesitate to send me an email at cyril@wslb.com.au

PERSONAL EFFICIENCY: THE FOUNDATION

1

PART ONE

1

❝ I often say 'the problem with common sense is that it is not commonly practised.' So it is with efficiency and effectiveness, the 'obvious' benefits are there yet even those with vision often lack clarity and focus.

General Manager Advice & Distribution
ING Australia

Chapter 1

WORKFLOW MANAGEMENT: DON'T LET INFORMATION SLOW YOUR PERFORMANCE

Six weeks per year

Let me tell you about a very interesting survey published several years ago in the *Fast Company* business magazine. The findings noted that, 'On average, white collar workers spend six weeks per year looking for information they already have.' We are talking here about the average worker, not particularly disorganised people, and about information they already have.

This is about the document we received via email a while ago and we are looking for. We scroll down in our inbox, going quickly through hundreds of emails to search for the document, getting more and more frustrated because we do not find it. We then realise we probably saved this document in one of our multiple sub-folders. We open a few, unsuccessfully trying to remember.

We then vaguely remember printing a copy of it. We go through our desk, searching through files of papers, with no success.

How many of us can relate to this?

I certainly could. I am naturally a hoarder, and was finding it hard to throw things away and therefore it was difficult to find things.

When I work with executives of large companies, one of the first things I ask them to do is to tidy their desk and their soft files. It is sometimes very challenging for these highly paid executives to suddenly have to go through all their documents and carry out a big purge, prune and file. But when I ask them if getting at least two or three weeks back per year by having a more organised filing system is worth the effort, they suddenly agree it's worth it.

The idea is to implement a workflow management system that will make you more efficient. You will save a lot of time and will be more focused on the information you really need — the information which will help you to progress in your role, not the things that could distract you.

Let's be clear on what we are about to do. We are about to completely reorganise your filing system. We are about to start a big purge and prune of all these documents on your desk, in your filing cabinets and deep drawers, in your personal drives and email folders. We are about to get rid of all those documents you do not need.

We are about to decide what filing system will work for you and agree on a few rules to make sure you will keep on top of it forever. And when I say forever, I really mean it. At Work Smarter: Live Better we have worked with many people and we often come back to visit them a few months or even years after, pleased to discover that the vast majority of participants have kept on top of their filing system.

1.1 HARD FILES – A CLUTTERED DESK, A CLUTTERED MIND

Let's start with your hard files, i.e. your paper documents, manila folders, files and binders. This might appear quite obvious; however people very rarely have an efficient desk. And most of the time re-organising their desk has an immediate impact on their focus and performance.

The aim is not only to do that big purge and prune, but more importantly to implement habits and behaviours that will stick forever.

Now, relax and breathe.

This is easier than you think because you only have to follow three steps:

- Step one: think
- Step two: sweat
- Step three: organise

Step one is about thinking of the most efficient filing system for you, a filing system that relates to how you think, how you view your role.

Step two is about sweating. It is the big purge and prune where you will review each document, throw out a few and file the rest.

Step three is about organising. Once you have reviewed all your documents, you can decide on an efficient filing organisation: what goes where, best cabinet or location, labelling everything and so on. This is quite easy as most of the work would have been done in step two.

STEP ONE: THINK

Great. I can feel you are now excited by the prospect of having an efficient filing system, by getting rid of all this clutter on and around your desk. Before you rush into it, let's take a few minutes to consider a few suggestions and design a system which will work for you.

A filing system so logical and simple you will be tempted to use it

The first principle in organising an efficient filing system is to design a structure, a backbone that speaks to you. Your filing structure should relate to how you see your role, to the different hats you are wearing in your job.

Your filing system should be so logical and make sense for you that it will be easy to respect and maintain.

Let's take the example of a sales manager. The different hats he (or she) is wearing could be:

- **Management** — management of his team

- **Key accounts management** — he is in charge directly of a few accounts

- **Marketing** — he is in charge of all the marketing activities such as leads creation, sales materials, etc.

- **Strategy** — he is involved with the sales strategy. He is also involved, along with the management team in the company strategy and vision

Each hat could be divided in sub-hats. This can be translated as this table:

Role	Hats	Sub-hats
Sales Manager	management	per name of person
	key account management	northern region — then per alphabetical order
		southern region — then per alphabetical order
	marketing	per activities such as advertisement, partnerships, website …
	strategy	per year

Figure 1.1: Structuring your filing system

What is key here is to choose names — 'hats' — that speak to you. You could have two people doing exactly the same role in the same company, yet their ways of seeing their role and responsibilities might be slightly different. One might call one of his responsibilities 'sales' where the other one might call it 'business development'. There is no right and wrong. What is important is to choose names which make sense for you.

I suggest spending ten minutes carefully thinking about your role and your different hats. You do not have to do it perfectly. What you are trying to do is a first draft. This will probably evolve as you start purging and pruning your files, as you will bump into documents and information that will add to this structure.

This will be the backbone of your filing structure. It will be used for both your hard and soft files. This backbone will be key during step two when you will purge and prune all your documents. You will use Post-it® notes and put them on each document with their hat and sub-hats. I will come back to this but this is a very important step of the process.

Labelling each document with its hat and sub-hat is key to the success of this process. You cannot have an efficient filing system if you do not label it well.

Be ruthless — avoid information overload

Before you launch yourself into step two, it is worth underlining how important it is to avoid information overload.

In today's business world, we are bombarded with information. Compare the number of stories and ideas which we must absorb each day to the often repeated claim that there is more information in one copy of a Sunday newspaper than the average person would have come across in the 18th century during their whole life. Whatever the statistics, with the rate of information growing at an exponential rate, we are under far greater pressure these days than we have been at any time in history.

Some of my clients receive hundreds of emails a day and have to read about a hundred pages a day. Talk about being swamped with information!

The key is to be very selective and very strict about what you will read and keep. You need to learn the difference between the 'must read' and 'must keep', i.e. information vital for our performance and the performance of our company, and the 'nice to keep'. Too often we spend time reading 'nice to read' information, or hanging on to 'nice to keep' material.

Remember the survey which found that we waste on average six weeks per year looking for information we already have. You need to be very harsh with your information, and only keep the 15-20% which is key for you; those things that are a 'must have'. Whenever you wonder if you should keep it, use the following guidelines:

1. Be honest. Ask yourself, 'Will I need it?'

If you don't think you will need this information in the future, and you do not need to keep it for legal reasons, throw it out.

The problem is that most people answer this question with, 'I might need this in the future.' The 'I might' is the answer of many hoarders who are buried under documents and information. They cannot throw things away as one day they 'might' need it. So go further and ask yourself these two questions:

2. When was the last time I used it?

3. What is the worst thing that can happen if I throw it out?

If nothing dramatic will happen when you throw it away or you have not used this information in a while, *chuck it*. Do not think twice.

I remember coaching a marketing team of a large bank. When purging the office, one of the managers uncovered a huge pile of documents which had been kept in one of her office cabinets. All documents had been written more than ten years ago. She had never looked at them, and had no reason to keep them. They were just there in case someone 'might' need them one day. Needless to say, she got rid of all of them.

Be smart and ask:

4. 'Can I find it easily somewhere else?'

How often do we keep a document we can easily find on our company intranet, on the internet, or that someone else in the company is keeping? If you can find it easily, don't hesitate, get rid of it.

If you bump into a hard copy of a document and you can easily retrieve the soft copy, don't clutter your paper files, chuck it. Now the easily is key. If you have a fifty-page colour printed document that would take a while to reprint from the soft copy, then keep it; that's fine.

There is an interesting figure to keep in mind whenever you manage information: **85%**. My business experience shows that 85% of what people keep they will *never look at again*. That relates to both our hard documents and soft files: 85% of the documents we keep in our folders, we will never look at again. And my experience as an effectiveness coach definitely confirms that.

For most of us, this is also true in our personal life. Those things we keep at home, in our garage, in our wardrobes and cupboard, in our storage area — 85% of all this we will never use again.

The important thing, though, is not the 85% that constitutes the clutter. The problem is the 15% of worthwhile information we crucially need which is hidden amongst the 85% we don't need. It is the document we desperately need and can't find in the middle of our 'organised mess'.

Again on the personal side, have you ever done a big purge and prune in your house and rediscovered old clothes or objects you love but had completely lost sight of among the rest … the 15% of your possessions that you value, hidden and therefore unused?

I keep a personal tally of the most impressive team of hoarders I have coached. So far the gold medal goes to a team of fund managers in one of Australia's leading banking and insurance companies. In one session with five people, we chucked four-and-a-half large wheelie bins of documents. Nearly a whole wheelie bin per person. Impressive.

In the 1980s, a Brazilian company called Semco had budgeted $50,000 to buy new filing cabinets. Semco CEO Ricardo Semler could not believe they needed to spend so much money to buy filing cabinets.

Rather than authorising the expense, Semler decided instead to stop the company for half a day and organise a big purge and prune. Everyone was involved, including Semler who had four filing cabinets and had requested additional ones.

After the purge Semco did not order $50,000 worth of filing cabinets. In fact they did not order any filing cabinets; they auctioned many of their existing ones. After the purge and prune they binned so many unnecessary documents that they were left with more cabinets than they needed.

From that day, Semco decided to hold a biannual file inspection and clean-up day.

STEP TWO: SWEAT

Group your files by frequency of usage

When you are doing your purge and prune, you will need to go through every document, decide the ones you want to keep and decide which 'hat' and 'sub-hat' is relevant for them.

I also suggest segmenting your files into four groups:

■ Working files

These are the files you use frequently, on a daily or weekly basis. They should be within hand's reach. You should not have to move from your chair to get to them. It's not so much the waste of time to stand up and get these files which is the problem. If your filing system is too hard to respect, your files will end up staying on your desk.

■ Library files

These are files you might refer to on a monthly basis. You do not use them frequently, but they are part of your library, of the documents you want to keep and might refer to from time to time. Your library should be close to your desk. You might have to stand up and walk to a filing cabinet to get them.

■ Shared files

How often when I coach people at their desk do we bump into a document they keep because someone else might need it. And my question is always the same: 'How would anyone know this document is there, hidden in your personal mess?' If you work in an office with colleagues, have an area for shared files and put documents to be shared in this area.

■ Archives

These are for documents you are unlikely to refer to, but need to keep for legal, compliance or corporate history reasons. You need to keep these documents but you are comfortable if they are stored in a different place, even in a different building. Archive files should be well organised and stored in a safe place.

The main point to remember in all this is simplicity and of ease of use. Your filing system needs to be so simple and easy to use that you *will* use it, even under pressure.

If you have or had young children, you will understand the following point. Keeping a room tidy with kids is almost impossible. My wife and I might tidy the house and it only takes a few minutes for the kids to bring it back to chaos.

I remember spending some time with each of my kids when they were at kindergarten. Impressed at how tidy the place was, I realised how easy it was to tidy, how simple the filing system was. In one corner there was a box for cars with a picture and a label on it; in another corner some large shelves for construction materials; in a third place a box for Lego, again well labelled. It was so simple that even a kid could understand the system and use it.

This is how your filing system should be: so simple and easy to use that you are tempted to respect it. I have a variation of the acronym KISS — keep it stupid(ly) simple. And yes, I do prefer it that way around!

Let's do it

Now is the time to be brave and review all your documents. When I say all, I mean all. I suggest you review all the documents on your desk, in your deep drawers, in your cabinets, on the floor ...

Do not underestimate the time that this will take. In my experience it will take about half a day. But I guarantee it is worth the effort. I have done this exercise with many people, and the smile on their faces at the end of the session, and when I come back a few weeks later, speaks for itself.

For this process you will only need the document where you wrote your hats and sub-hats as suggested back in step one ('Think'), some Post-it® notes and a pen.

Now, clear some floor space ready for what you are going to do.

Take the first document on top of the first pile. Here is the process to follow for every document. I repeat: *for every document.*

1. Ask yourself, 'Do I really need this document?' Review the principles of 'Be ruthless, avoid information overload.' Put it in 'my friend the bin' if appropriate.

2. If you decide to keep this document, look at your hats and sub-hats, decide upon the appropriate hat and sub-hat, write it on a Post-it® and put that sticky note on the document.

3. Decide where on the floor you will place your working documents, your library documents, your shared documents and your archive documents. Create four different 'zones'. Decide whether this document is part of your working, library, shared or archive zone. Then place it on the floor in the right area.

Use this process to review each document. If you already have a document on the floor with the same hat and sub-hat, you do not need to rewrite a Post-it®; simply put the new document with the one of the same category.

You may think that this process might be a bit laborious — I agree. A CEO told me one day, 'The first two hours of purging and pruning was quite easy and fun. After two hours it is becoming harder, boring and laborious.' Still, I encouraged him to continue. I came back two weeks later for another session to hear this CEO thanking me. 'I have now a much more efficient filing system. It is easier to find documents and I don't waste time doing it. I am glad you pushed me to do the purge and prune.'

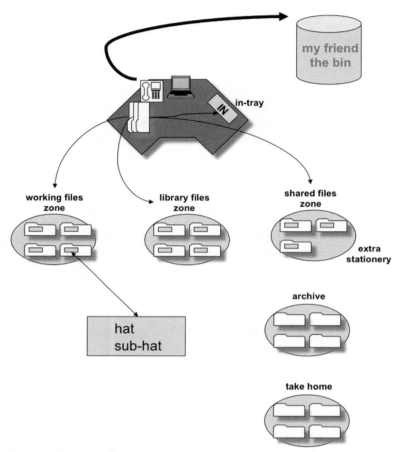

Figure 1.2: The purge and prune process

STEP THREE: ORGANISE

After going through all your documents, checking what you will not need and labelling the rest on the floor, your office will probably look like a real mess with paper everywhere. Don't worry; this is absolutely normal. If you have done the process right, and have labelled everything, the next step will be quick and easy.

Before you move everything back to your desk or filing cabinets, let me emphasise a few simple and important principles.

KISS — Keep It Stupid Simple

As mentioned earlier, a good filing system is a simple one. If it's too complex, it will be hard to respect it and as soon as you come under pressure you will slip back into old messy habits.

Here are a few 'keep it stupid simple' suggestions.

You have probably heard about the old principle 'A place for everything and everything in its place.' This applies well to your filing system. You should have a place for all your documents and materials, and make sure you put things back once you are done with them. Otherwise you will lose time looking for things.

Sunday afternoon. You have been invited for lunch with the kids. After much effort the kids are finally ready to go. You look for the car keys on the key holder, only to realise the keys are not there.

For the next five minutes you look everywhere, wondering if you or your partner dropped them somewhere in the house, or if one of the kids played with them. It's a waste of time and it's frustrating.

It's the same in our work place. How much time do we waste looking for documents which either have not been put back where they should be or do not have a place where they should be? So, have a place for everything and label it well. I repeat this, as it is important: label, label, label.

Imagine you are away from your office and have forgotten a very important document. You should be able to call one of your colleagues, even someone who is from a completely different department and has no idea about your role, and ask him or her where to find this document without any hesitation. You filing system needs to be so simple and well labelled that anyone can find documents very easily.

Cluttered desk, cluttered mind

I am always impressed by the impact a clean desk has on people. And often until we work with them they do not realise it — in fact, they think the opposite. They believe a messy desk means you are very busy and active. They think an empty desk means you are doing nothing.

How wrong, in my opinion, that is.

Don't get me wrong. I am not in favour of an empty desk. I like a desk with personal objects and pictures — those little things which make you feel at ease while sitting at your desk, those things which enhance your creativity.

What I fight against is the messy desk with piles of documents and notes everywhere, and where you can hardly see the colour of the desk. There are two reasons behind it. A messy desk invites distractions and lack of focus. And a messy desk creates stress and lack of concentration.

We will discuss later the impact of a big time waster called lack of focus. In our business world today we are constantly breaking our concentration. You start working on something important, and your eyes skim to a document lying on the side of your desk. You suddenly remember you have to finish this document today; that someone has been chasing you for this.

You either stop what you were doing and start this new task, or come back to your original task, but have broken your train of thought.

You go back to your important project and, a few minutes later, notice a small Post-it® on the side of your desk. Without even thinking about it you quickly read the note: 'Call Jan regarding project W.' You remember now that you had promised to call Jan yesterday and you've forgotten. Again, for a few seconds, sometimes a few minutes, your attention moves away from the key project you are working on. You either call Jan or continue your important work, but with the guilt and stress in the back of your mind about the phone call you should have made.

Let's be clear. Our desks have not been designed to be our task management system. However many people use their desk as such. They keep documents and notes on their desk to remind them that they have to do something. A desk is a poor task management system. It does not tell you when something is due or how long it will take. It does not prioritise.

You have a much better system called Outlook (or Lotus, or …). We will discuss this further on in this book.

In the introduction I mentioned that I take pictures of the desk of people that I coach, first before the start of our journey and then afterwards. I could have written a book just with these pictures — some of them are unbelievable. How people manage to work and concentrate in such a mess is a mystery.

Filing back

You are now ready to put each document back. Have a look at the amount of documents in your **'working file'** zone on the floor. These documents should be filed within hand's reach of your desk. Have a look at the amount of documents in your **'library'** zone. These documents do not have to be within hand's reach but should be within a few steps of your office desk.

By this stage it ought to be quite obvious where to put each file. If you have a deep drawer under your desk, this is a good place for your working documents. Try to avoid the divider system on your desk. If you have a filing cabinet in your office, this is a good place for library documents.

In some cases, you will have to order a deep drawer or the right filing cabinet. But in my experience this is quite rare. In most cases, we have more space than we need. Like the example of Semco, most people have too many documents before this process, and end up at the end of it with a lot of free space.

So take each pile of 'hat and sub-hat', label according to your system and place it where it belongs.

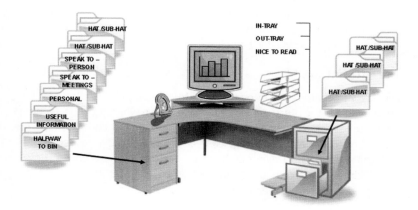

Figure 1.3: Placing files

1.2 SOFT FILES: THE INVISIBLE MESS

Although I sometimes hear from someone with a messy desk that they have an 'organised chaos' and that they know where everything is, most people agree that a messy desk is not a great sign of efficiency. And the ones with messy desks are often claiming that 'one day', 'when they 'will have a bit of time' or 'after Christmas when business is quieter' they will purge and prune their desk.

However most people don't realise the same inefficiencies are also true for soft files. A messy desk is visible. It annoys and distracts you. While a messy soft filing system is less visible, the time wasted to look for soft documents is probably greater than hard documents as we are, more and more often, working onscreen. Most of the time the name of the document is not enough to let us know whether it is the document we are looking for. We need to open it and check what is inside.

The different soft files

Let's define what we mean by soft files for the purposes of this chapter. Most people in the office use a desktop or a laptop which is connected to a server. The server could be a physical one in their office or another office, or it could be a 'virtual server' accessed over the internet. On their computer they can store soft documents in their local hard drive (often called 'C drive' on Windows-based computers) and emails in programs such as Outlook or Apple Mail®, or in a web-based collaborative application such as those provided through Google. On the server, they can store documents in a personal drive (often called folder) or in shared folders. They are the only person to be able to access their personal folder, whether the shared folder is accessible by all or only by a selected group.

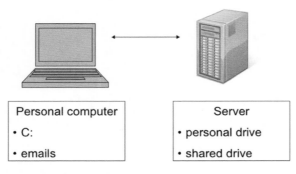

Personal computer	Server
• C:	• personal drive
• emails	• shared drive

Figure 1.4: Soft file storage

In this chapter we will only discuss rules to efficiently manage your personal folder on the server and your emails in your computer.

Your computer's hard drive — be aware of the 'when' not the 'if'

As one IT professional mentioned to me, a computer crash is not a question of 'if' but 'when'. You are likely to experience computer failure one day, with the risk of losing all the information in your local hard drive (or 'C drive'). Retrieving this information might prove to be impossible or at least difficult and time-consuming.

I do not recommend keeping any soft documents on your local hard drive as it is either not backed up or it is time-consuming to back it up. Most companies do not have automatic back-up for the local hard drive of their employees.

If you have to keep soft documents in your local hard drive because you either don't have a server with a personal drive or are travelling a lot and need your files regularly, implement a routine to back up your information often, ideally daily at least weekly.

Most medium and large companies have automatic back-up procedures. However if you are working for a small business or from home, your files might not be backed up automatically. Make sure you save your files regularly. A small USB or thumb drive is very handy although should not be relied upon as it is also liable to failure or, more likely, loss. There are also many web-based free online storage services that allow you to backup your files.

Shared folder/drive — same logic as a group

I will concentrate on your personal soft files rather than your shared documents. In most companies you can file your soft documents in the server, either under a personal drive or folder or under one or several shared folders. We will discuss how to be more efficient with your personal folder in the server, not the shared folder.

Having said that, the same logic applies to the shared folder. The only difference is that you need to organise the purge and prune as a team. The team needs to decide on the right filing structure, on the naming policy and finally on who will purge and prune what.

The two simple steps

Re-organising your soft file systems is actually quite easy once you know where to start and what to do. It takes only two simple steps:

- Step one: Implement
- Step two: Purge and move

STEP ONE: IMPLEMENT

The same filing logic

I suggest using the same filing structure that you have defined earlier for your hard files. The logic we used was to start with your role, to think about your hats and sub-hats. There's no need to redo this. You should use this logic both for hard and soft files.

Implement means you need to implement this structure for your soft files. You need to create the right folders (within your personal folder on the server or within your email program). They will be empty to start with, and in the next step you will move all your files into the newly-created folders.

Order your folders

I suggest putting numbers at the start of each folder. If your main hats are management / business development / marketing / strategy / operation, your filing structure will look like this:

1. Management
2. Business development
3. Marketing
4. Strategy
5. Operations
8. Personal
9. Archive

This will be very useful in the next step, when you will purge and prune all your existing soft files. By putting a number in front of each new folder, they will come at the top of your filing structure, of your filing tree. I have deliberately used the numbers 8 and 9 for 'Personal' and 'Archive' to leave room for any new folders that might be required after '5. Operations'.

If after doing the purge and prune, you want to get rid of the numbers, that's no issue. However I find that most people enjoy ordering their folders, putting the most used ones on top.

Halfway to the bin

When it comes to your email, I suggest adding a new folder on top of your structure: Halfway to the bin (HWB).

HWB is a folder I use a lot. When I receive an email that I don't need to keep in the long term but would like to keep for a few days, the HWB folder is where I keep it. For example if I receive flight details for a trip I will do in a few days, I put all the relevant information in my calendar, but keep the email until the flight is done. Once my trip is over, I can delete the email.

Do you need an archive folder?

To prepare for the next step — purge and prune of your existing soft files — it might be useful to create an archive folder. All the existing folders or documents that you are unlikely to use but feel uncomfortable deleting could be placed in this folder.

Your archive folder could just be a dumping ground with not a lot of structure or organised by dates, by hats or by previous roles. It is for you to decide what will work best for you.

STEP TWO: PURGE AND PRUNE

Now that you have implemented your 'ideal' structure with your relevant hats and sub-hats, it is time to do a purge and prune of your existing soft files. Because you have numbered your new folders, they are on top of your structure. All the previous folders and soft documents are below this new structure:

1. Management
2. Business development
3. Marketing   ⟵ new filing structure
4. Strategy
5. Operation
8. Personal
9. Archive

Action
Cathy Simon
Clients
Finance
John Smith   ⟵ previous filing structure
Johnson & Johnson

Marketing
Meetings
Merrill Lynch
Project XYZ
Strategy

Go to the first previous folder, in the example above it is 'Action', open it and check the documents inside. Decide which documents are relevant or not. Delete the ones which are not relevant. Once you have reviewed all the documents, decide where this folder sits in your new structure.

A few possibilities may occur:

■ You may decide that the whole folder is obsolete, and delete it;

■ You may decide that you are unlikely to use it but do not want to delete it. You can move the whole folder into 'Archive'; or

■ After purging and pruning the documents inside, you may decide these are relevant documents and move the whole folder into one of your new folders.

In my experience this is a very quick and simple way to re-organise your soft files, both emails and under your personal drive.

The right amount of time spent purging

How much time you need to spend on each folder and each document depends on how useful it will be in the future.

If you have many soft documents, most of which you need to use often but are lost in your filing structure, it is probably worth spending time doing a thorough purge and prune. If your previous filing structure is clear and you know most of the documents inside, you do not need to open each document to check. You may want to just move the previous folders into your new structure.

Use your common sense for this.

How many levels of sub-folders?

Under each hat, you can create different sub-folders and even for each of these sub-folders, you can create sub-sub-folders. For example:

Business development
    XYZ Pty Ltd
        Overview

Meetings
Proposals
etc ...

How many levels you need depends on how useful each will be for you and how easily you will be able to find the information you are looking for. If you have five documents under 'Business development' you do not need sub-folders. Finding one document among five is easy. However if you have one hundred documents under 'Business development' you will probably save time when looking for one of them if they are organised in sub-folders.

Speed and ease to use is what I am after here. Again, use your common sense to decide how many levels of sub-folders you need.

Be ruthless

We keep far too many documents. This is true with hard documents as discussed previously; this is even more valid with soft documents. Emails are a great example. It is so easy to file an email, and because we think, 'You never know, I might need it,' most people end up keeping almost every email they receive.

Remember the survey regarding hard files. Eighty-five per cent of the documents you keep you will never come back to again. Well, based on my experience of helping many people with their soft files, 95% of the emails you keep you will never come back to again.

Be ruthless in deciding upon which information you will keep. Remember the simple questions to ask yourself:

- **Be honest**   'Will I need it?'
- **Be ruthless**   'When was the last time I used it?'
  'What is the worst thing which could happen if I throw it?'
- **Be smart**   'Can I find it easily somewhere else?'

Delete the soft documents you are unlikely to need in the future and only keep the few (5-15%) you will really need.

Simple and clear names

I am often asked for advice on naming policies for soft files. This is an important point as the name of a soft document is all you have to assess its content. In contrast, you can visually scan a hard copy of a document and so know quickly what the document is about.

Very often when I coach someone as they purge and prune their soft documents, they have no idea what content is in a soft document. They see a name and it does not ring a bell, then they need to double click on the document to open it, wait until the software is loaded on their computer, wait for the document to open and then scroll through it to figure things out.

Multiply this by the number of documents they look for every day, and it becomes quite time-consuming.

So when it comes to labelling a document, my main recommendation is to give a name so clear and simple that you don't have to open the document to know exactly what is inside.

I suggest the following simple naming policy:
date – type of doc – name of doc – person.

So, for example, a proposal created by John Smith on 25 October 2010 for Apple's offsite in March 2011 would look like:
'2010 10 25 – proposal – Apple offsite 11 March – John Smith'.

Avoid duplicates

There might be a few documents you could file in two different folders. For example, you may have a document related to the delivery of a specific client order. It could be kept under the client file in your 'Business development' hat or under another file in your 'Operation' hat.

You could be tempted to duplicate the document and keep one copy in 'Business development' and another in 'Operation'. It is very easy to 'copy and paste' a document and create two copies of it. I strongly recommend against this.

If you keep two copies of the same document, you may end up with two hybrid documents with relevant information in both. Let's say after a while you decide to add some information to this document and update paragraph one of the document kept in 'Business development' and paragraph three of the document kept in 'Operation'. You have now two hybrids of the same document, neither of which is accurate.

Decide once where it is most logical to file a document, and stick with it.

1.3 FEEL THE DIFFERENCE

The impact of an efficient filing system is often underestimated. 'I know I should tidy my desk but I do not have the time and, besides, I can find anything pretty easily.' Remember, though, the six weeks per year on average that we spend looking for information we already have.

When people claim to be able to work with a system of 'organised chaos', it makes me smile. As I coach people at their desk over a period of a few months, often there comes a time when I am with them and they search desperately for a piece of paper or an email. After hunting for a few minutes, they look at me, I smile, and they do as well. And then they admit, 'Ok, Cyril, you have a point.'

People do not realise the impact of their inefficient filing system until they have experienced a genuinely efficient one. I will never forget Bob, a manager from a worldwide financial institution. After a few sessions we had completely reviewed how Bob was managing his information. We had carried out a big purge and prune and implemented a new filing system.

As I was leaving, Bob shook my hand. He said, 'I have been working in this organisation for many years and I realise now how stressed I was at my desk. After just one session, you have completely changed that. I feel so much better, it is incredible. Thank you.'

I have many, many examples of people who have been so relieved with their new filing system. One lady said to me, 'I didn't realise I had a cluttered desk so I had a cluttered mind.' As a marketing manager of a large bank, being able to concentrate at her desk to be creative was key for her and her role.

Do not underestimate the importance of an efficient filing system. You will save a lot of time and feel far less stressed. The four hours' pain of purging and pruning is really worth the gain.

2

❝ I now have a method of systematically planning my time and I get more done, I have a significantly increased sense of calm and organization. I am much more protective of my time and this means I don't allow people to waste it.

Head of Marketing
Asgard Wealth Solutions

Chapter 2

EFFICIENT BEHAVIOURS: THE WORK HABITS OF 'DOERS'

A slim difference with a huge impact

It is interesting to see what makes the difference between a procrastinator and a doer. In my experience the difference is only a few simple behaviours. But the difference in the end in terms of both output and outcomes is a huge abyss. I can speak with expertise on this subject. First, because I have helped a lot of people over the years in this area but, more importantly, because I was one of them. I was a procrastinator.

To tell the truth, I was a perfectionist. And the separation between a perfectionist and a procrastinator is slim. Very slim. I could not start a project or a task because I did not have enough time in front of me to do it properly. My inbox was full of emails that I wanted to do 'perfectly' later and my head full of ideas that I would do 'one day, when the time is right.'

The reality is that the time was never right and I didn't suddenly have lots of time to do 'perfectly' all I had to do. So I was procrastinating. Then I realised procrastinating was just a habit and that moving to the opposite direction — becoming a doer — was simply a habit as well.

As mentioned, the difference in action is very small, as I will explain later on. However the difference in outcome is huge.

Have you ever worked with or met a real 'doer', a real entrepreneur in the spiritual sense of the word? A 'doer' actions things quickly, prefers doing things even imperfectly rather than waiting for the best time to do them, and gets things moving by their level of energy and commitment.

It is amazing to see how much more they achieve per day compared to other people. It is amazing to see how many more emails/tasks/projects they go through per day. And when you bring that to a year of achievement, there is a world between them and other people.

And the difference at the end of year is inspiring. It's not that they are working harder or more hours. In some cases, they work less hours. It's just that they have a different attitude to work.

In my experience, the difference lies in a few habits and mind shifts. It lies in their ability to:

- Avoid wasting time on low-impact or low-value activities; and

- Make quick decisions, go for the 80% right now rather than the 99% perfect later.

The three time wasters

I want to share with you a few simple habits which could make a world of difference in your day-to-day effectiveness. However, make no mistake: although what I share is very simple, transforming it into a habit is hard and requires commitment. It requires consciously thinking about it and practising it for 21 days.

Remember the strange lottery I explained at the start of this book? It illustrated that most people place a lot of value on money, but fail to understand the value of time. We waste our time on things that are not important to us, to the detriment of what is key for us.

Every day we allow our time to be stolen and we do not react. Time is far more important than money; however we place little value on it. How often do I hear people saying they wish they had more time with their loved ones, time to exercise, time to enjoy life? What is more important than your partner, your kids, your family, your health, your passions?

When discussing this with our clients in small and large business, we often hear people say they work hard all day but have not spent any time on the few 'big-ticket items' which will ultimately impact on their performance.

Their days are full of 'emails', 'interruptions', 'crises' and 'irrelevant meetings' to the detriment of the few things which are key to their long-term performance.

Over many years I have observed and fought against three major time wasters in organisations: procrastination, lack of focus and ineffective meetings.

Understanding is easy. Changing is not

The principles I will explain below are simple. They are, in fact, so simple and so easy to understand that you will be tempted to read through, believe you can easily master them and fail to take action.

Understanding these principles is easy. Practising them until they become new habits, however, is hard. Believe my years of experience as an effectiveness coach — so often I have people in our workshop nodding as I explain these principles, only to struggle when we practise them back at their desk.

2.1 AVOID TIME WASTER ONE: PROCRASTINATION

How many times do you handle the same information?

Monday morning. You get to your office, grab a cup of coffee on the way and switch on your computer. Your first reflex is to open your inbox and check your emails. You read the first one, then the second one.

The third message is an important email from a key client. You need to work on it before replying, and this will take a bit of time — probably around an hour. You have a good read and decide you can't do it now but will have to come back to it later on today.

The day goes with its usual number of crises, interruptions and meetings. You have been quite busy and time has flown without you realising it. It's now the end of the day and you are finally about to go home.

Just before closing your computer, you glance quickly at your inbox. Suddenly you look at that important email from your client. For the second time you read this email carefully. You can't do it now as you are about to leave, but really want to work on it first thing tomorrow.

To make sure you will not forget, you print the email and put it on your desk.

Tuesday morning, same routine. You grab your coffee, get to your desk and see the printed email sitting on it. For the third time you read the message. You remember that you need to spend a good hour on this but realise you have a meeting in fifteen minutes. You put it down again, thinking you will have to do it later.

How many times do we open and read an email before actioning it? How many times do we take a document on our desk or in our in-tray, read it and decide to come back to it later? How many times do we remember something we need to do, think about it and decide to do it later?

What you are doing is called 'multiple handling'. You are handling emails, papers and thoughts many times before making a decision and taking action on that.

And the time waster behind this is called procrastinating. We procrastinate on both small tasks and large projects. When the deadline finally arrives, we suddenly run in panic mode, get stressed and are at risk of running out of time to deliver as expected.

The impact of procrastinating is quite serious. It can have an impact on our performance. We are at risk of either missing the deadline or of doing a rushed job, working far less effectively than we should.

Procrastination also has a big impact on our stress level. This might surprise you, but I really believe stress at work is not linked to the amount of work we have. To be clear, I repeat: stress is not linked to the amount of work we have. Stress is linked to the way you manage your workload.

I have seen high level executives who have huge amounts of responsibilities and big workload but are feeling in control and relatively unstressed, and I have also seen very junior people with a much smaller workload being completely stressed and feeling out of control.

Stress is linked to how you manage your work. It is, for example, being home in the evening but still thinking, or even worrying, about all the things you should have done — the phone calls you have made, the unfinished tasks with close deadlines. If you have an efficient system to organise your priorities and you have made a decision for each of them, you can dramatically reduce the amount of stress.

As mentioned earlier, the process to go through in order to move from being a procrastinator to a real decision maker is simple. But changing it into a new habit is hard.

Two simple steps: batch and decide

■ Batch = schedule and do not check in between

I suggest that you group similar tasks such as inbox management, in-tray management, invoice management, etc …

For example, decide and schedule a few times per day to check your emails. In my opinion, less is best. Most people check their inbox far too often. Once or twice a day should be enough except for some specific jobs.

Outside of your scheduled time to check emails do not open your inbox. Do not look at your email. This is easy to understand but so hard to apply. We are so used to 'butterflying' with our emails — to check a few, do something else and come back a few minutes afterwards to check a few others.

Be strong and strict. Decide when it's time to check emails or to check the documents in your in-tray, and in between, do not look at it. A simple way to avoid the temptation to check emails is to remove the new mail alerts. In Outlook, click on Tools – Options – Email options – Advanced email options and adjust the settings so that no audio alert is activated, and no 'new mail' envelope icon appears on your screen.

When it's time to check your emails, become a 'processing machine'. You aim is to process as many emails as possible in the time you have scheduled. This brings us to the next steps:

■ One touch = one decision

This is probably the most important principle, in my view, regarding efficiency. It makes the difference between the real doer of the world and the rest. If you can practise this principle until it becomes second nature, this will be extremely valuable.

The logic is simple. You need to make a decision as soon as you touch an email or a document, or think about an idea. It does not mean you need to do it, you just need to decide what you will do and when.

The chart below explains in simple steps what to do.

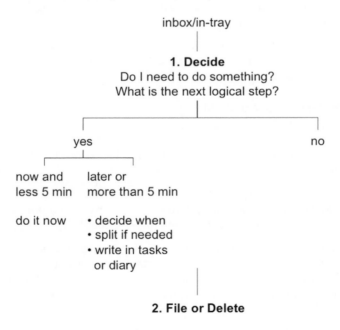

Figure 2.1: Inbox/in-tray flow

Let's explain using in-tray management as an example. When it's time to check all the documents in your in-tray, take the first one and do not put it back, or file it, or look at the next document, until you have made a decision.

Ask yourself, 'Do I need to do something with this?' If this answer is 'yes', simply ask yourself, 'How long will it take?'

If the answer is less than five minutes and you can do it now, then do it now. If it's a document you need to read and you can do it in less than five minutes, do it now. If it's a phone call you need to make to someone, and it will take less than five minutes, go ahead and do it now.

If the answer is less than five minutes but you cannot do it immediately, then decide when you can do it, and schedule that. 'Attention!' as I would say in French; only if you really cannot do it now. For example you need to call someone but you know this person is on leave until next week. What you need to do is decide when you will do it, and schedule it in your Calendar or Task function (more on this in the section on Outlook).

If the answer is more than five minutes, then don't do it now but decide now when you will do it, and schedule it. Estimate the amount of time you will need, go into your calendar and book a meeting with yourself at a specific date and time.

Once you have made a decision either to do it now or schedule it now, remove the piece of paper from your in-tray.

Same logic for an email. Once you have made a decision on an email in your inbox, the email needs to be removed from your inbox. Either delete or file the item.

In my earlier example of the email read on Monday morning, Monday afternoon and Tuesday morning without taking action, the best way to handle it would have been to ask, while reading the message for the first time, 'Do I need to do something about it? What is the next logical step?'

As it was an email that required some time, the next question ought to have been, 'How long do I need to spend on it?' Knowing that the email required an hour's preparation time, the next step should have been to open my calendar, decide when to do it (for example next Wednesday from 10:00 am until 11:00 am) and diarise it in my calendar. Then I should have either deleted the email or filed it where appropriate.

The one-way street logic

Think about your in-tray and inbox as a one way street system. Once you have touched an email from your inbox, the email is not allowed to stay there. You need to make a decision and either delete or file the email. Once you have touched a document in your in-tray, the document is not allowed to go back in the in-tray. You need to decide on what action is required and then either bin or file the document.

Let me guess. When you arrive home at the end of the day and check your letterbox, do you stand in front, take the first letter, open it, read it, put it back in the envelope and then return it to the letterbox thinking, 'I need to do something about this; I'll keep it there and do it later'? Then do you take the second letter, open it, read it, put it back in the envelope and then back into the letterbox thinking, 'Interesting information which might be useful one day. I'll keep it there in case I might need it.'

I would hope not. You do not use your letterbox as a 'to do' list or a storage system. Why do we do this with our inbox for emails and in-tray for documents? Remember the one-way street logic: once you have touched a document in your in-tray or an email in your inbox, you need to make a decision and take it out.

Don't let the spark become an inferno

If you procrastinate on many things, you are likely to run into a few crises. This is what I call the spark which becomes an inferno. If you had dealt with this email straight away or with this paper straight away, the crisis often could have been avoided. But by leaving it in your inbox or in-tray for too long, you are facing a crisis.

You might relate to this example: you have had a little pain in one of your teeth for a while. It's not big and it comes and goes, so you don't bother about it. You say to yourself, 'It will probably go away. I'll be fine.' And, for a while, you are right. You are fine.

Then a few months later you wake up in the middle of the night in incredible pain. You are up for the rest of the night and rush to the dentist first thing in the morning. Now you need a serious treatment. And of course you hear the dentist saying, 'It's a shame you did not come to see me a few months ago; this would have been far easier to deal with.' And far cheaper as well.

You ignored the early signals and let a spark run into an inferno. Rather than procrastinating, you should have asked yourself immediately, 'Do I need to do something about it?' You would have answered, 'Yes, go and see the dentist.' What is the next step? Call and book an appointment. How long will it take? Two minutes. DOING IT NOW would have made a lot of difference in the end.

Transform this into a new habit

Be strong on this over the next few days. It is a difficult habit to gain as we are so used to multiple handling. When I work with a small team, I discuss this principle in a workshop and ask people to go back to their desk afterwards to practise. How many times have I heard people saying it was easy, only to find out when I join them back at their desks that they are struggling to do it.

Here I am with them coaching them at their desk. They are practising the principle we have just discussed. They take the first email and either act on it or make a decision on when to deal with it, then the second one. But often after a few 'easy' emails to process comes a difficult one. They look at it, think about it for a few seconds, find it too hard and close it saying, 'I will come back to this one later.' I have to gently remind them what we agreed about the one touch = one decision rule. They laugh, I laugh, and they return to the email to make a decision.

After practising this for a few weeks, it slowly becomes second nature.

I have seen people, whose inbox was completely out of control, being transformed by this principle. Some of the people I coach receive thousands of emails each week, and felt stressed just by looking at their inbox, knowing they had been procrastinating on making decisions regarding many emails. Suddenly they acquire this new habit, and their approach to email is transformed.

I have seen people with papers requiring action strewn all over their desk. Just looking at their desks and the number of undecided papers was enough to stress them. This new habit has transformed their life.

If you recognize yourself and want to change, be harsh and persistent with this for at least two weeks. Religiously apply the principles above for two weeks, and I guarantee you will start seeing the difference.

The 'do it now' habit is much more than a simple tactic for dealing with emails. It is one of the most important habits of doers, of people who make decisions and take action. Managing your inbox using this principle is a great way to practise this powerful habit. The aim is to then use this principle in many instances: with emails, with papers in your in-tray and, more broadly, with many decisions you will have to make.

2.2 AVOID TIME WASTER TWO: LACK OF FOCUS

Interruptions and distractions

Do you know the difference between an interruption and a distraction?

The difference is quite simple. An interruption is caused by someone else and a distraction is caused by you.

You are working at your desk and a colleague pops in to discuss something with you — that's an interruption. You are focusing on an important document and your mobile rings — that's an interruption.

You are working on a key project and suddenly you remember an email you promised to send to someone — this is a distraction. You are home playing with your kids but your head is full of unattended work crises — this is a distraction.

A state of high productivity

Try to remember a time when you were 100% focused. You got in to the office early in the morning before everyone, or you stayed late one evening when all your colleagues were gone, or you worked from a different location. There were no interruptions or distractions and you were very concentrated. You worked solidly for a while and suddenly looked at your watch. Two hours had passed and you did not realise it.

In these two hours you probably achieved more than you normally would in four hours. You were in a state of high productivity and high performance.

Interruptions and distractions pull us from a state of high productivity. They reduce both our productivity and performance.

Some interesting facts

As I mentioned earlier, in 2006 University of California (Irvine) researchers found that, on average, workers were interrupted by phone calls, text messages and people every three minutes. Every three minutes!

Another study published by BASEX in New York shows that, on average, white collar workers are spending more than two hours per day on interruptions, and this can go up to 50% of their work day.

And here is my favourite one. A psychiatrist at King's College in London did three similar IQ tests on one group of people. The first IQ test was done in normal and quiet conditions, in a room with no noise and interruptions.

The second test was done in a 'normal' work environment, in an open plan with interruptions, phones ringing and emails popping. The British sense of humour came into play for the third test. They made the group smoke marijuana and then did the test.

Not surprisingly the first test got better results than the two other ones. What was more interesting is that the test done after smoking marijuana got better results than the one done in a normal work environment.

Now don't make me say (or write) what I haven't said. Smoking marijuana is not my new technique for concentration. My point is that we have created a work environment which is less conducive to concentration and productivity than if we were completely stoned with drugs.

If you put these studies in parallel you realise the impact of interruptions on our productivity and performance at work. Our current work environment, with open plan design, emails and mobile phones, is dramatically reducing our concentration and focus. We would be better off smoking marijuana and working from home than working in our offices!

Here are a few simple suggestions to reduce interruptions.

Reduce interruptions — YOU decide

You are working on something quite important and one of your colleagues pops in for a quick chat. Rather than jumping into the interruption, ask the person to explain in twenty seconds what it is about. Then YOU make the decision regarding whether or not it's worth stopping what you are doing.

In some cases, there will be a good reason to accept the interruption. It could be a critical external or internal issue that requires immediate attention. However in most cases the matter is either not that important or can wait.

Rather than stopping the important piece of work you are doing, just ask the person to come back later when it suits you. If you know you will need another hour to finish what you are doing, it is totally acceptable to ask that the matter to be discussed in an hour.

You do not have to be rude by saying no straight away. Take the time to listen the person, and then YOU make the decision.

Reduce interruptions — batch communication

Rather than interrupting your colleagues regularly, or being interrupted by them, I suggest to batch communications with some of them and to use the 'speak to' logic.

With the people you need to communicate with often and regularly, such as your manager, your direct reports or some of your colleagues, you should set up a regular catch-up once a fortnight, once a week or even once a day for a PA and his or her manager.

For these people, I suggest then to create a 'speak to' document. This could be on a piece of paper filed in your filing cabinet, on a word document or on a note in your phone or PDA. If you meet on a weekly basis with David, create a 'speak to David'.

Whenever you think of something to mention or discuss with David, and if this can wait until the next catch-up, simply write it on your 'speak to David'. Before your next meeting with David, simply take or print your 'speak to David' and have it on hand at the meeting.

Organise regular catch-ups with the people you need to communicate often with and ask them to create a 'speak to' for you. You will be surprised to see that most of the interruptions can wait until the regular catch-up. Only a few are really urgent and cannot wait.

I remember the feedback of a director of one of the largest financial institutions in Australia. He had applied the logic of 'speak to' and asked his direct reports to do the same. After a few weeks he was amazed by the impact. He was far less interrupted than before.

And, in addition to dramatically reducing the number of interruptions from his team, he also found out that 50% of the issues his direct reports wanted to discuss had been resolved by the time they had the meeting.

Reduce interruptions — create 'non-interrupted' time

In our crazy busy business world we are often confusing speed for performance. Multi-tasking is a buzz word. We try to race through every day and respond to many emails, make many phone calls, squeeze in as many meetings as we can, go through many tasks …

Yes, speed and quantity are important. But this should not be to the detriment of quality, of thinking, of planning, of innovation. Most people say their performance would improve if they had more time to think, plan and focus.

We need to create time and space for quality time. We need to create 'non-interrupted time'. If you are working on a key project or doing something which will have a high impact on your business, turn off your mobile phone, divert your phone, close your inbox … and focus.

You might also have to protect yourself from the office interruptions. If you have an office, close your door. If you work in an open plan environment, agree on a signal to let your colleagues know you do not want to be interrupted. Some people put a red flag on top of their computer to indicate this; others put their iPod® earplugs in. In our office, the person in charge of our administration has a sign she puts on her chair that says, 'I am working on something important. Please do not interrupt unless the building is on fire,' with a picture of Rodin's statue *The Thinker*.

If this doesn't work, why not work from home once or twice a week, or book a meeting room and isolate yourself? I was coaching a regional executive who was constantly interrupted by people and phone calls, and was finding it hard to focus. She decided to work one day per week from home. After a few weeks, she realised she was doing more in one day at home than three days in the office.

Reduce distractions — capture/write it down

Although it is easy to blame others for our lack of focus, we are often our worst enemy when it comes to staying concentrated.

We start to work on something and suddenly remember a phone call we have to do. We either make the call and completely break our focus, or decide to do it later, and keep the idea playing in the back of our mind.

We continue working and in the document we are focusing on we see the word 'expense'. We suddenly remember that we have forgotten to submit our expenses to be processed and paid, and that the deadline for this is today. We either drop what we are doing to deal with our expenses, or we continue what we are doing but have this little 'expense stress' in the back of our mind.

Our subconscious mind could be described as an elephant in comparison to the little mouse of our conscious mind. We have thousands of ideas and thoughts going through our mind at any point in time, most of them in our subconscious. From time to time, one of these thoughts moves from our subconscious to our conscious and starts bothering us. We suddenly remember something we have to do. And we do not realise the stress attached to this.

If you are well organised and have a system you trust, your level of stress is reduced. All through this book I am making suggestions to implement a work system you will trust. Regarding distractions, the suggestion is 's.s.' or 'stupid simple': capture your thoughts. Write it down.

As soon as you think about something you need to do, simply write it down. Don't let the thought go back into your subconscious.

I suggest you use a 'collection tool' such as a mini notebook you carry with you all the time to write all these ideas. You can also use the note section in your BlackBerry® or iPhone® and create two notes, one called 'to do — office' and one called 'to do — home'.

Whenever you think about something you need to do, either during a meeting, while walking in the street or wherever you are, write it either in your 'to do — office' list or 'to do — home' list.

On a daily basis, review your 'to do — office' list while in your office. Apply then the '**one touch = one decision**' rule discussed earlier.

Reduce distractions — clean desk policy

When I am invited to coach someone, one of the first things I review is how they have organised their files and how they manage their information. We go through a big exercise of purging and pruning, and completely reorganise their desk.

You would be surprised at how many times I heard someone being amazed by the impact of a clean desk on their concentration. Suddenly their desk is organised and not messy. They only have one document on it — the one they are working one. Their concentration is so much higher and it takes them half of the amount of time to complete a task compared to what it would have taken them before.

Here's a scenario to illustrate trying to work with a cluttered desk: you are working on an important project. Suddenly you see a Post-it® on your computer 'email Sue'. You realise you are due to email Sue but have completely forgotten. You either write the email straight away, and break your concentration on your important project, or decide to do it later, but have this in the back of your mind.

You come back to this important project and do your best to return to the job at hand. Just as you get back into it, you notice another document on the 'to do' pile — your manager needs it taken care of today. But your day is already full of meetings and this job will take at least an hour. You're caught, not sure whether to stop what you are doing to get into this new task, or decide to do it later, not really knowing when.

Your hesitation leaves the problem at the back of your mind, generating low level stress as you wonder when you will be able to get that job done.

I hear people saying, 'Cyril, this is all well and good, but if I put this Post-it® or this document away, I'll forget that I need to do it.' In other words, out of sight is out of mind. This means they are using their desk as their task management system. And believe me, your desk is a very poor task management system. Remember, it doesn't tell you when to do something and how long it will take. Outlook is a much better task management system. We will discuss a bit further how to use Outlook as an efficiency tool.

I am not suggesting you should have a 'clinical' desk, i.e. an empty desk with nothing on. I like a desk with pictures and personal objects. We spend hours at our desk, so it should be a nice environment, an environment where you feel creative and you can focus and think.

2.3 AVOID TIME WASTER THREE: INEFFECTIVE MEETINGS

When am I supposed to do my job?

Most white collar workers spend many hours per week in meetings. An executive can spend as much as 70% of his or her time in meetings. I am not saying this is good or bad. I am just making the point that because we spend so much time in meetings we need to make sure they are effective.

In my experience this is an area which, in many cases, could be improved. I read a survey which mentioned that 50% of meeting time is wasted time. I often hear comments such as, 'The meeting was too long', 'It was a complete waste of my time,' and, 'We hardly spoke of the key topic.'

I remember a senior manager of a large group who showed me his calendar in his BlackBerry®. His weeks were full of meetings from 8:00 am until 6:00 pm. I will always remember his words: 'Cyril, when am I supposed to do my actual job?'

Value your time as much as your money

Remember the example I presented earlier: if someone asks you for $500, you would want to know why, and would need some good reason before giving the money away. We are constantly being asked for our time, to participate in too many meetings, and we are often happy to give our time away quite easily.

Be as careful with your time as you are with your money. Ask the reason for the meeting and try to determine whether this is the best value for your time. Ask for an agenda before committing; do not simply accept a meeting request. With technology it is now so easy to organise meetings through Outlook or another online method. This can be quite dangerous.

It is simple to click on 'accept' when you receive a meeting invitation via email. Don't. Question the value of any meeting before joining.

You can put a dollar value on your time. Calculate your business fees (salary, super, bonus and so on) and divide them to get an hourly fee. This will give you an idea of what you are giving away when you accepting a meeting.

Less is best — eliminate

The most important advice regarding effective meetings is also the most simple: eliminate unnecessary meetings. You need to be protective of your time, and carefully select the meetings you will accept.

I know it is easier to say than to apply. But if you have worked with highly effective and successful people, you have probably noticed that they will question the aim of a meeting and ask why they should be there before deciding to go.

Keep this in mind: whenever you are saying yes to a meeting, you are saying no to something else. The one or two hours you will spend in this meeting are gone forever. They could have been spent on a much more important project, which would have had much more impact on your performance.

So one of your key tools here is the word 'no'.

To reiterate: if you are invited to a meeting, ask for the agenda before accepting. Then make the decision. Is it worth your time? Would there be a better use of your time?

And if you decide to go, assess the right amount of time needed. We often book one-hour meetings, or in multiples of one hour. I have often thirty-minute meetings and even forty-five minute ones. It is interesting to see how, when you give a shorter time frame, everyone gets more quickly to the point.

Stick to it

During the meeting, make sure you stick to the agenda. There needs to be someone in charge, 'chairing' the meeting to make sure the meeting keeps on track.

A simple rule for an effective meeting is to start with the most important items. It is very frustrating to have a meeting, go through many minor items, and only start discussing the very important one ten minutes before the end. You either rush an important discussion or decide to spend more time than planned, to the detriment of other things you had planned to do afterwards. Sometimes you may even be forced to arrange an additional meeting as a result.

Be proactive

After a meeting, make sure you take five minutes to plan your next steps. The five minutes afterwards is just to make decisions, not to action what you have to do. You may have committed yourself to a number of tasks, both large and small, during the meeting. Remember the five minute rule.

If planning all your tasks will take less than five minutes, do it now straight after the meeting. If it will take more than five minutes, decide when you will debrief the meeting and book a time with yourself in your diary.

Be also proactive in suggesting changes for regular meetings such as weekly team meetings or monthly committees. Whether you are the organiser or a participant, don't hesitate to suggest a change to the format of the meeting. Could it be done more effectively using a different format? Is the length of the meeting appropriate? Is the frequency right? For example, rather than a one hour weekly meeting, would it be better to have a one-and-a-half hour meeting fortnightly?

In a previous role I was in charge of a team located all around Australia. We had agreed on a weekly phone hook up every Monday morning for one hour. Every quarter the main topic for the meeting was, 'Are we wasting our time during this meeting? Should we change something?' I wanted this meeting to be of value to everyone, a meeting people would look forward to. The best way to do this was to ask everyone what they wanted and how we could make this time effective.

2.4 EFFICIENT BEHAVIOURS: AWARENESS

The above suggestions regarding how to avoid time wasters are simple and easy to implement. However the first step in reducing time wasters is to recognize their ugly heads when they appear. As one of my clients once said a few weeks after our first coaching session, 'I don't know if my work behaviours have improved yet but what I know is I feel so guilty now when I procrastinate, multiple handle, distract myself or get interrupted by someone.'

Be honest with yourself. With the previous time wasters in mind, write down which time wasters are the most applicable to you. Identify your biggest two or three.

Once you are clear on this, write down what do you need to do to improve. Improvement does not have to be complex. Simple strategies as outlined before are enough to get big results.

Efficient work habits are a very important step to feeling in control. If you are disorganised and not as efficient as you could be, you will pay a double penalty. First you will take more time to achieve what you need to. You will waste precious time. As one manager wrote to us after we had coached his team:

> *'The increased focus of the team accelerated some key projects by approximately six months. It is hard to quantify the impact on the revenue and performance, but I know it is huge.'*

The second penalty you will pay is the impact on your stress and your work-life balance. As mentioned earlier, stress is not linked to the amount of work we have to do. Stress is linked to the way we handle it. I have seen CEOs with a huge number of responsibilities being relatively in control, and junior people being completely stressed with their work.

Stress is going back home in the evening, being physically at home with your partner and kids, but mentally still in the office. Stress is thinking about this phone call you did not do, this report you did not finish, this email you did not send.

I say this often, but I am always amazed to see the impact of a clear desk on someone. Many people I coached have been working for years in a semi mess. After our first session, they cannot believe how relieved they feel and how much more concentrated and productive they are at their desk. They suddenly realise they had created a work environment full of distractions.

3

❝ All the items and clutter on my desk and in my in-box was distracting me and causing my attention to flip from one thing to another. This has given me the tools to clean and organise my desk, my in-box and ultimately my mind.

Financial Controller
Macquarie Bank

Chapter 3

OUTLOOK AS AN EFFICIENCY TOOL

People use many different ways and tools to keep on top — or to try to keep on top — of what they have to do. Some people keep many notes and documents on their desk to make sure they remember to do it. They fear 'out of sight out of mind', so if they do not see the document they need to work on, they will forget to do it.

Others write everything on 'to do' lists and papers. They end up with many lists of things to do. I have seen a few interesting 'Post-it® strategies' where the desk or the computer is covered with Post-it® notes. Others do not concern themselves with notes — they pretend all is in their head and they will remember everything. Most people use a combination of the above.

And we wonder why we forget things or struggle to achieve all these on time. In this section, I would like to show you how Outlook can become your efficiency tool.

Remember that I don't believe your desk is a good task management system. Keeping documents, notes and 'to do' lists on your desk to remind yourself you have to work on them is not the best system. Your desk does not bring your documents to your attention when it is the right time to do the task. Your desk really is a very poor task management system.

I don't believe our brains offer a great task management system either. Don't get me wrong, I believe our brains are great for thinking and for creativity. We still have not found any tool which is better for innovation and thinking. However our brains are poor time and task management systems.

If I ask my brain to remind me in three weeks on Tuesday at 2:00 pm to call Gary, I cannot guarantee that I will remember it exactly at that time. I will probably remember this at a completely unexpected time — under the shower or when I am playing with my kids. I cannot guarantee that I won't completely forget about it until Tuesday 2:00 pm in three weeks' time.

If I ask my brain to remember all the meetings I normally put in my calendar, with the date, time, name and location for every meeting, and to remind me just before each meeting with the right information, I really cannot guarantee I will not forget something.

You need a tool to be efficient

I am not advocating Microsoft Outlook above other personal management systems such as Lotus® Notes, Novell GroupWise, a smartphone or PDA application, or a paper diary. All can be great efficiency tools and the principles below are as relevant for any of these tools. However, as Outlook is the tool that most people use, I will focus on this. Outlook is a productivity application that has been available as part of the Microsoft Office for Windows suite for many years, and is now (2011) available on the Macintosh platform as well.

Most people use Microsoft Outlook mainly as an email management tool, with their Outlook open all day simply for emails. They use their calendar mainly, if not only, to record external meetings. The 'Task' function is either not used at all, or is full of red tasks left undone.

Outlook can be far more than this. As Peter Drucker, one of the most famous consultants in the space of effectiveness and performance, wrote, 'What gets measured gets managed.' Outlook can and should be your efficiency management tool.

My aim is not to become too technical or IT savvy. This would bore you — and me — to death. I will explain how Outlook can be used as an efficient task management system and show you the few tips and tricks which will be useful.

I will focus on three areas of Outlook:

- Inbox: Who manages who?
- Filing: Efficient system versus growing dump
- There is a life beyond Inbox: Calendar and Task

3.1 INBOX: WHO MANAGES WHO?

When coaching people at their desk, I wonder sometime who the master is and who the servant is. Many people are completely swamped with emails. They have not seen the white space at the bottom of their inbox for a long time. I often see people with several hundred emails in their inbox and regularly people with several thousand. Several thousand …

Imagine someone with thousands of items of mail in their letterbox at home, many unopened.

We are receiving more and more emails every day. Think how many emails you received ten years ago — probably less than ten per day — and how many you receive today. On average, people receive 40 to 50 emails per day. Some of our clients receive up to 200 emails a day.

The fun and excitement of receiving emails is long gone. It's now a rat race that most of us are losing. The more emails we check and deal with, the more we receive, and so the more time we need to invest each day.

People are now checking their inbox first thing in the morning, all through the day with their inbox permanently open, while going to meetings (and even during meetings on their phone) and back home in the evening or on weekends, either via their phone or webmail.

The average worker is now spending more than an hour per day on email. Some interesting terms have been created recently …

■ **Inboxicated:** Feeling sick when our inbox is reaching its capacity.

■ **Spamnesia:** Regularly forgetting to delete spam and junk emails resulting in our inbox overflowing.

Hence my question: who manages who? Are you on top of your emails or are you losing this rat race?

Avoid email interruptions

Many people view email as a great progress of the last few years. We cannot imagine doing business without emails. And in truth, emails are very useful if used well. What we are starting to realise is the price we are paying when we are not using this tool properly.

I noted on page 8 the results of an Australian survey that found, on average, that people are checking their emails 50 times per day.

Now, I cannot verify the survey so cannot guarantee the figure. What I know is that people are constantly looking at their inbox. Most of the time the inbox is open on their screen, and it's hard to resist to the temptation to check our emails very often.

You start working on something at your desk. Suddenly you hear the alert sound of a new email arriving. Automatically you have a quick look to see who it is from. Or you are working on a document on your computer, and the 'new mail' envelope icon appears suddenly on the bottom right of your screen. It doesn't stay long, but long enough for you to see who it is from and the subject. Long enough to get distracted.

You continue working on your project. It's an important project but a hard one. After a while, you start fading down and decide to check a few emails instead. You do not feel guilty because you are still working. Checking emails is part of your work, and you receive so many emails per day that you need to keep on top.

But are you really being effective and productive?

Between interruptions from colleagues, distractions from the office when working in an open plan and interruptions from new emails, how much concentration do we give to important work, how much focus do we give to critical projects?

You might recall the survey done by King's College in London (*see page 54*). All this put together, our work environment today is making us less productive than if we were completely stoned with drugs. And emails are a big part of it.

Remember a time when you were 100% focused. You suddenly looked at your watch and realised two hours had gone in a heartbeat. You were in a state of high focus, of high productivity. This is what we break all the time by jumping on emails as soon as they arrive.

Batch and do not check in between

The first rule to manage your emails efficiently is simple: batch email checking time. Schedule a few times a day and DO NOT LOOK AT YOUR INBOX IN BETWEEN.

The less, the better. You should try to check your inbox only once or twice a day. Of course this will depend on your role. Some roles require checking emails more often. However the more senior you are the less dependent on emails you should be. I doubt that your organisation is paying you for your ability to respond to emails.

By the way, by batching emails and making decisions as soon as you touch one as suggested in the previous paragraph, you will have far more chance to be on top of your emails.

Do not check emails at random. Decide that you will check your inbox only a few times per day, for example at 11:00 am and at 3:00 pm, and do not check in between. Close your Outlook or leave it open on Calendar, not at your inbox. You need to adopt with Outlook a 'calendar centred logic' and not an 'inbox centred' one.

Turn off the alerts. Do it now. Go to Tools, Options and in the Preference tab click on Email Options/Advanced email options. Then under 'when new items arrive in my inbox' deselect or un-tick all the options. Otherwise you will be interrupted every time a new email arrives, either by a sound or by the envelope icon at the bottom right of your screen. If you are receiving on average sixty emails per day, this means many interruptions per day.

Don't let emails become another ongoing distraction

Do not underestimate the disruptive impact of emails on our concentration and focus. There are many sources of interruptions and distractions in our workplace today, and emails are only one of them. But they are a powerful one.

After discussing this, some of our clients decide to work regularly from home, for example once a week. They are not interrupted by colleagues and decide to only check emails once or twice during the day. They all report a massive increase in productivity. In one day they get through what would have normally taken them three days to complete in the office.

You need to detoxify yourself from the email habit. We have become email junkies. We check our inbox many times per hour. And when we are not in the office, we now have our BlackBerry®, iPhone® or other PDA devices, to make sure we can receive emails whenever they arrive. We are also completely used to 'butterflying' with our emails, checking one with taking no action and 'butterflying' to another one without doing much on that one, either.

Most people today would suffer to a certain degree from the above habit. If you recognise yourself there, you need to go through a detox. Be disciplined. For the next three weeks, apply the above principles every day. Be conscious of it every day and force yourself to respect these principles. After two to three weeks you will start creating new habits and it will become second nature.

Don't spend time on low value-adding emails

I often ask a simple question to the people I coach: out of ten emails you receive, how many will have a long-term impact on your performance? And the average answer is one or two, maximum. This means 80-90% of the emails we receive will have no or little impact long-term on our performance. It does not mean we should not respond to them, but it does mean we should not spend too much time on them.

Firstly, remove yourself from all unnecessary email lists. If your email address has been around for a while, or if you regularly subscribe to different sources of information, chances are you are on the emailing lists of several organisations. Be very harsh with the time spent on these. Make the difference between the 'nice to read' and the 'must read'.

Get rid of the 'nice to read'. You could spend your all day reading these documents without any boost to your performance. Unsubscribe from all 'nice to read' email lists. Focus only on the 'must read', on that information which is critical to your success/performance. Organisations should offer an option at the end of the email to unsubscribe. If this information is a 'nice to read' and not a 'must read', unsubscribe yourself. You do not have time for 'nice to read'!

Be also very harsh with the amount of time you spend responding to emails. Doing well something which is not worth doing is a complete waste of time. You look at an email in your inbox, and realise you would ideally need thirty minutes to respond properly. Ask yourself if the quality of your response is important and if it will have an impact on your performance.

If the email is not that important, if the impact on your performance is low, spending time on it is not effective. You are better doing a 'quick and dirty' response in five minutes rather than writing the perfect answer in 30 minutes. You are better using this 30 minutes for a more important topic.

I can relate well to this as I was, and probably still am, a bit of a perfectionist. My inbox was full of emails I was keeping there waiting to have the time to do the 'perfect' answer. Either I was spending too much time on these emails, to the detriment of more important tasks, or I was forgetting about them. A quick and dirty answer would have been much better than no answer at all.

Reduce time spent on cc

The number of emails we are being sent a copy of is becoming an increasing problem in large companies. One of my colleagues was working with a CEO who was fed up with being copied on many emails. There was a strong 'copy all' culture in this company, some people would say a strong 'cover my a…' culture, and it was having an impact on the number of emails everyone was receiving.

In Outlook you can easily set up rules. In this case, the CEO decided to implement a simple rule. Whenever he was cc-ed on an email, Outlook automatically deleted the email without him reading it and automatically sent an email back saying: 'You have cc-ed me on an email which has now been automatically deleted without me reading it. If you want me to do something, could you resend the email TO me and explain clearly what I need to do?'

As a result he reduced the number of emails he was receiving by 70% and sent a strong message to the whole company. Of course this is easy to do when you are the CEO and probably not as easy to do if you are not. But it shows that many emails we are cc-ed on are not important for us.

There are other less extreme ways of reducing the time you spent on cc-ed emails. If you are cc-ed on many emails, and realise that many are probably irrelevant or will have little impact on your performance, you could create a 'cc folder'. You can create a rule in Outlook to automatically move all emails you are cc-ed in a specific folder and checking them quickly once a week. As long as this cc folder does not become a procrastination folder, and as long as you have the discipline to check it once a week, this could be a good way to reduce your time.

Let me explain quickly how to set up the 'cc folder rule' in Outlook. Here are the simple steps to follow:

- when in the inbox, under Mail, click on Folder Tools/Rules and Alerts

- click on 'New Rule' and select 'start from a blank rule'

- select 'where my name is in the cc box' and 'Next'

- select 'move to a specified folder'

- also select 'have server reply using a specific message'

- in the second step, click on the word 'specified', click on 'New' and create a folder called 'cc folder'

- also in the second step, click on 'a specific message' and type message, for example: Thanks for your email. As I was cc-ed I assume it is only for information and not for action. To free as much time as possible for key projects I only read my cc once a week. However if this email is urgent or for action, could you be so kind to resend it 'To' me and let me know clearly what I need to do. Thanks for your understanding and help.

- click 'Next'

- decide if there will be some exceptions and click 'Next'

- give a name and click 'Finish'

- schedule one hour per week to check your received cc's, and stick to it

I was coaching one of the general managers of a large telecommunications operator. He was receiving many emails every day, many as a cc. We created a 'cc folder' and a rule to divert all cc emails in this folder. A few weeks later he mentioned how well this was working for him. He was checking his 'cc folder' once a week and realised that there were only one or two important emails in it out of fifty to one hundred emails.

Another suggestion to reduce the number of emails you are receiving — both cc and others — is to educate your team. If you have many direct reports and they have a tendency of inundating you with emails, set up the 'two bullets per day' rule.

Tell each member of your team that they are only allowed to send you, either To or cc, two emails per day with only one topic per email. If the topic is not important, they should not send it to you. If the topic can wait your regular catch-up, they should put it in their 'speak to' list and discuss it with you face to face. This will force them to think about what they really need to send you, what can wait for your regular catch-up and what they should manage by themselves without involving you. And it will considerably reduce the number of emails you are getting.

Avoid email procrastination

A very big danger with emails and inbox is procrastination. The example of multiple handling emails given in chapter two (see page 48) explains it all. It means reading emails and then leaving them to sit in your inbox without making any decision.

We look at an email, and decide to come back to it later. We look at a second one, decide we need to 'sit on it' for a while, and leave it in our inbox. We take a third one, a difficult one, and start thinking about it. Suddenly the phone rings, and we leave this email to focus on something else.

I exaggerate a little bit here — we do not doing this with every email, but I know a lot of people are procrastinating with emails. You just need to have a look at the number of messages open and undealt with, still sitting in their inbox.

Poor email management creates stress, wastes time and reduces our performance. An important email which could have been done quite easily early on can become a big crisis if left undone. Deadlines can be missed, delays can be created, and stress builds up.

One touch, one decision

Fighting against indecision is both very simple and very hard. The fight is simple because the process to manage your emails efficiently is very simple. Yet the difficulty lies in the fact that most people have to fight against years and years of bad habits: of procrastinating with their emails, of 'butterflying' with their inbox. Too many people put off the making of decisions, and jump quickly from one email to another.

Here is the simple process — I do use the identical diagram as the one on efficient work habits, as it is crucial to email management. Allow me to impress it upon your memory:

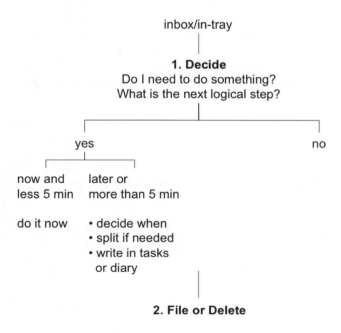

inbox/in-tray

1. Decide
Do I need to do something?
What is the next logical step?

yes   no

now and   later or
less 5 min   more than 5 min

do it now   • decide when
                 • split if needed
                 • write in tasks
                   or diary

2. File or Delete

Figure 3.1: Using the inbox/in-tray flow for Outlook

When you are checking your inbox, you are simply making a decision on each of the emails in there. When reviewing an email, you need to answer the simple question: 'Do I need to do something about it, and what is the next logical step to deal with this email?' If you do not need to do something with it, either delete or file the email.

If you need to do something with it, ask yourself the second question: 'How long will it take me and can I do it now?'

If it will take you less than five minutes and you can do it now, then do it now. Do not procrastinate — send the response or forward the message to the right person with a request for action, e.g. 'Please action this.'

If it will take you less than five minutes but you cannot do it now, schedule a time in your task management system when you will do it, then either delete or file the email. You need to be honest with yourself that you really can't do it now. For example, you need to check a website but are not connected to the internet. Or you need to call someone but you know that the person is not available now. It is, 'I really cannot do it now,' and not 'I could do it now but could do it later as well'.

If it will take you more than five minutes, open your calendar and decide when you will do it. Block the time in your calendar and then file or delete the email. Some people argue that it is hard to know exactly how long it will take to do some tasks. I can understand that, but procrastinating any action is not going to solve it. You are better off making a rough estimation and scheduling the time instead of saying to yourself, 'I will do it later when I will have the time.'

If you recognise that this is an area of improvement for you, and you really want to change some of your work habits on dealing with emails, be harsh with yourself for a few weeks. As soon as you have read an email, do not allow yourself to check another one before you have made a decision on this email and moved it out of your inbox, either into your Task, Calendar, Contacts, folders or the bin.

The key to managing your inbox is immediate action. That sounds easy, but I can guarantee this will be hard. You will check a few and all will be good. And then you will bump into the difficult email, the email you want to sit on for a few days so you are tempted to leave in your inbox. Push yourself and make a decision now on what is the next logical thing to do.

After practising this for a few weeks, it will become second nature.

Put your processing hat on

When it is time to check your inbox, your aim is to become a 'decision machine'. First email: make a decision (do it now or decide when and schedule that action) and move on. Second email: make a decision and move on, and so on.

The aim is to process as many emails as possible during the time allocated to check your inbox.

You need to picture yourself with two different hats, two different attitudes. The first hat, or attitude, is the processing hat. Your aim is to process as many things as quickly as possible. The second 'hat' is the thinking hat. When you have your thinking hat on, you are not after speed but quality. You want to be focused and concentrated.

When you are dealing with your inbox, you want to wear your processing hat. Your aim is to make decisions on as many emails as possible in the shortest period of time. You are the postman in front of a big pile of mail, triaging each letter into the right box. Some emails will go into the bin; others into your filing system, others will be moved to your Calendar or Task system to be done later, while others will be dealt with quickly and then sent back.

Many people try to wear both hats at once when they check their inbox. That is a mistake. They try to process emails and then bump into an email to which they need to reply. They swap hats, put their thinking hat on, and spend time considering how to write the answer. Do not put your thinking cap on. Just decide how long it will take you and when you will do it.

If you decide you need to spend one hour on something sent via email, write in your Calendar when you will do it, for example Wednesday at 11:00 am, and move on to the next email. On Wednesday at 11:00 am, put your thinking hat on and spend the time on this topic.

Moving emails into your Tasks, Calendar or Contacts

Most people know how to move an email from their inbox into their folders. But many people do not know that a great feature of Outlook is allowing you to move an email into your Task, Calendar or Contacts systems.

Let's say you have decided it's time to check your inbox. You have cleared thirty minutes and the aim is to process as many emails as possible. You plan to make a decision on every email you will handle and move each from your inbox.

The first email is a monthly report you need to read. It will take you a few minutes to read it. DO IT NOW — open the attachment and read the information. Then either delete the email or file it where appropriate.

Second is a message from a colleague asking for some information. You decide it's best to call him to clarify exactly what he wants. If the phone call is likely to be quick, DO IT NOW. Pick up the phone and make the call straight away.

Third is a request from your boss who needs your input on an important project. You estimate you need a good hour to work on this. DECIDE WHEN NOW. Have a look at your calendar and decide when you can do it. You can then drag and drop the email into the calendar folder or display button of Outlook Calendar. This will open a calendar entry and you just have to write the relevant subject, then choose the date and time.

The fourth message is from a client who would like to talk to you next week about a proposal. You cannot do it now as the client as specifically requested you call him next week. However, you can drag and drop this email into the task folder or display button of Outlook Task. This will open a task entry and you just have to write the relevant subject, then choose the date and time.

When you drag an email into your Outlook Calendar or your Task, this will only copy the body of the email, not the attachment. I do not recommend dragging attachments into Task or Calendar as this will decrease the space available on your Outlook. However there might be a few cases where this could be of benefit.

An easy way to do this is to right click on the email and to drag it into Calendar or Task. This will open a box dialogue from which you should choose 'Move here as Task or Calendar with attachment'.

Another way to move an email to Calendar or Task is to right click on the email and select 'Move to Folder'. Be aware that this will entirely move your email with its attachments. The email will be gone from your inbox.

Again my aim here is not to transform you into an Outlook guru. It is to show you that Outlook can be a great efficiency tool to organise your tasks and priorities. Nowadays we receive so many requests and tasks via emails that being able to link emails with Task and Calendar is very useful.

I will address Task and Calendar in more detail later in this book.

You can also drag an email into Contacts. Outlook will automatically create a new contact with the right name and email address.

What your Inbox should not be

I have seen so many people with inbox full of emails, from hundreds to thousands. And when I ask why they keep all these emails in their inbox, the answers vary from 'I did not have the time to do it', to 'I want to keep this email', to 'I keep it as a reminder of something I need to do later' to 'I want to keep the contact details of this person.'

Let me be clear on what inbox is not:

▪ Your inbox should not be a filing system

When pointing to some read emails in their inbox, I hear people saying, 'I don't need to do something with this email but would like to keep it.'

First you need to make sure you really need to keep this email. Remember the principles described on page 27. Will I need it? When was the last time I used this information? What is the worst thing which will happen if I delete this email? Can I find this information easily somewhere else?

Be harsh. Only keep the few emails you really need. If you really need to keep it, your inbox is not the right place to do so. Create folders in Outlook and file your email appropriately. See the next paragraph regarding filing.

▪ Your inbox should not be a task management system

When pointing to some emails in their inbox, I hear some people saying, 'I need to keep this email as I have to do something about it.'

Your inbox is a poor task management system. It does not tell you when you need to do it, whether you have the time available that day, or how long it will take. You have a much better way to manage what you have to do in Outlook with Calendar and Task. More on this a little bit further, in the paragraph on Calendar and Task.

▪ Your inbox should not be a contact management system

When pointing to some emails in their inbox, I hear some people saying, 'I need to keep this email as I need the contact details of this person.'

Your inbox is a poor contact management system. You can argue that you can search your inbox by name, but when you sort your inbox by 'From', the senders can be displayed by first name, last name or, even worse, by how their email address is spelled. Often you waste time searching this way. You have a much better way to manage your contacts in Outlook Contacts. Not only will your contact be found more easily in Outlook, but for those using a device such as BlackBerry®, iPhone® or other smartphone, all your contacts will be synchronised in your device.

■ **Your inbox is not a bin**

If I could get one dollar every time someone I coach has deleted an email in their inbox which was sitting there for no reason — which had been read and dealt with but not deleted — I would be a very rich man.

Be ruthless with your emails. Once you have dealt with it by either taking action or scheduling some action, file or delete the email. Do not keep it in your inbox. Your inbox is not a bin.

Inbox should only be a receiving system. Your inbox is just a notification you have received new information or requests which have not been dealt with. It is just a receiving system, as is your mailbox at home.

As mentioned in the previous chapter, you do not leave your mail in your mailbox at home. You do not use your mailbox at home to store interesting information you have received or important letters you need to act on. Well, it's the same story for your inbox. It is only a receiving system and should not be anything else.

ADVICE ON WRITING EMAILS

1. Emails should be short and to the point

I find long emails quite difficult to read. Of course writing a concise email is often harder than a long one. To quote Mark Twain, the famous American writer of the 18th century: 'I am sorry I had to write you a long letter. I didn't have time for a short one.'

I find the 'four sentences' rule works well: answer all emails in four sentences or less. If you require more than that, it should be a new email from you to the sender for a different topic, or probably shouldn't be an email at all. Consider phoning the person to go over the material in more depth.

2. Label the message with an explicit subject

Be as clear as possible. Rewrite it if necessary, explaining the subject and the reason of the emails. For example: 'Your feedback on the XYZ marketing project' or 'Information to read in preparation for the offsite'.

3. Leave white space

Write small paragraphs with one line space in between. If you have received long emails without spaces in between paragraphs, you know how hard they are to read. I suggest writing a few lines, and then spacing it with one line before the next paragraph.

4. Be clear on the purpose of the email

Probably the most important advice is to be clear on the purpose of the email at the beginning. Sometime you receive a long email. You spend a few minutes reading it without really knowing what you need to do. Why did that person send you this email? Is it for information only? Are they expecting an answer? What exactly and by when?

It would have been much more efficient to start the email with the aim. Something like, 'Dear ..., Could you do this by this date?' Then explain the story and why they are involved. The person will understand from the start what is expected from them.

5. Avoid cc-ing the whole world

It is so easy to cc people today that we are sometimes abusing it. Imagine cc-ing a large document to fifteen people who each would take five minutes to read the message. You have suddenly dedicated seventy-five minutes of the company's time to this one topic. It might be relevant and important, but if it's not, it's seventy-five minutes of lost productivity. This might sound a bit extreme, but when you multiply this by the amount of copied messages going around, there are some serious productivity gains to be made by limiting the number of people we include in cc. Not only is extra time taken reading these copied messages, but some recipients will feel it is necessary to reply in acknowledgement, further adding to your inbox clutter.

USEFUL TIPS

Here are a few tips I find helpful in Outlook. I have only selected those which are the most popular and useful. Be aware that Outlook can do much more than this.

Signatures

When sending an email or replying to an email, Outlook can automatically insert your signature. To create it, click on Tools/Options/Mail Format/Signature/New. You can then create a few different signatures and decide whether you want to use a particular signature only for new messages or also for replies and forward.

Distribution list

If you send emails regularly to the same group of people, you can create a distribution list. This will avoid having to type each email address every time you send a message to this group. You type the group name into the 'To' bar, and Outlook will automatically send it to all the people associated with this group.

To create a new distribution list, click on File/New/Distribution List. Choose a name for this group, for example 'Marketing Team' and then click on 'select members' to select all the people associated with this group.

Colour emails

Outlook enables you to colour all the emails received from a specific person. If you are receiving many emails every day, and would like to highlight all the emails received from a few specific people, you can do this quite easily.

Simply click on Tools/Organise/Using Colours. Then, in your inbox or in your folders, click on an email from the person. This will select the name of the person, for example 'Steve Smith', then choose a colour and click on 'Apply Colour', for example red.

From now on, all emails in your inbox from Steve Smith will be coloured red.

Searching

From time to time, you might be frustrated because you cannot find a specific email. You are pretty sure you filed it somewhere, but where? You can search quite easily in Outlook. Click on Tools/Find/Advance Find. You can search all emails either received from or sent to a specific person. You can also search using a specific word from the subject or inside the message of the email.

For example if you are looking for an email related to a specific project named 'project alpha', you can search for all emails with the word 'alpha' in the message. Pretty powerful.

Of course, if you have purged and pruned and reorganised your filing system, this should rarely be needed …

Out of office

This tool is only available if your Outlook is on an exchange server. If you are in an office with several users, you are probably on an exchange server. If you are working from home on your own, you almost certainly are not.

If on an exchange server, you can activate the 'Out of Office' assistant when you are on leave. For example if you go away on leave for a week and do not want to check emails while away, you can activate your 'Out of Office' assistant. Whenever you receive an email, an automatic reply will be sent with a pre-written message. For example, you may want to send a reply saying, 'I will be on leave until the …. and will have limited or no access to my emails. For any urgent matter, please call my colleague Amy Smith on … .'

To activate your 'Out of Office' assistant, click on Tools/Out of Office Assistant and fill in appropriately.

For those who are fed up with coming back from leave to hundreds of emails, and who are still resisting the growing trend of checking your emails via your BlackBerry® or iPhone® every day while away, here is a suggestion which might save you a lot of time and stress.

In the 'Out of Office' message sent while you are on leave, you could try something like this:

'I will be on leave until (date) and won't have access to my emails while away. In order to avoid being inundated with "out of date" emails when I am back and to be quickly back on focusing on important matters, all emails that are received while I'm on leave will be automatically deleted. If the matter is important, could I ask you to resend this email on or after (date). Thank you for your help in making me more productive.'

It's a little extreme but it would dramatically reduce your stress and time wasted when you are back.

Security

A few words of caution. First of all, regularly save your email folders and inbox. An IT specialist once said to me regarding computer failure, 'It's not a question of if, it's a question of when.' One day you are likely to experience computer failure or problem. So back up your data regularly.

In most medium to large companies, this is automatically done. However it is worth checking with your IT department or IT provider if it is done or, if not, how you can do it.

The other thing to be mindful of is viruses. Do not open any attachment unless you are confident it is safe. Even if it's an email from someone you know, but looks suspicious, do not open the attachment. Send an email back to the person to check it's not a virus before opening it.

3.2 FILING – EFFICIENT SYSTEM VERSUS EXPANDING DUMP

Most people understand the link between a cluttered desk and a cluttered mind. With some reason we wonder how someone who has a messy desk can concentrate and be on top of his or her priorities.

The same dangers exist with soft files in Outlook. We regularly coach people with thousands of emails in their inbox and an email filing system where they struggle to retrieve emails when needed.

My question is simple: do you have an efficient filing system for your emails in Outlook, or do you have an expanding dump?

I am not going to suggest you spend hours purging and pruning your email folders if it's not worth it. If you have a good system, i.e. if you can retrieve any emails you have filed very quickly, keep it.

However, if you waste time looking for emails you filed, then it might be time to review your email filing system.

In my experience, the quickest way to reorganise your email filing system is similar to the process described on page 36:

- **Step one: Implement.** Create folders based on the structure designed on page 38.

- **Step two:** Purge and prune existing folders/emails and move to the right location.

The same filing logic

If you have read and done part one (on hard and soft files), you do not need to spend any time on this. You already have designed an efficient filing structure, a filing structure that will work for you. If you have not done it, refer to page 26 and design your filing structure.

STEP ONE: IMPLEMENT

Step one is simply to implement this new filing structure into your Outlook. Create empty files based on the structure you have designed.

Let's take the example of someone managing a small business. The person has designed the following structure, the following hats:

- strategy
- marketing
- sales
- finance
- delivery/production
- administration

I suggest creating the following structure in Outlook:

01. halfway to the bin
02. strategy
03. marketing
04. sales
05. finance
06. delivery/production
07. administration
08. personal
09. archive

Halfway to the bin

This is probably one of the folders I use the most. We have a 'hoarder tendency' with emails. I often see people keeping nearly every email they receive. Except for specific jobs in legal and compliance, we do not need to keep most of our emails.

Remember, 85% of what you keep you will never go back to again. And I believe it is even more for email. In my experience, 95% of the emails we keep we will never go back to. Be harsh with emails; only keep the few, the 15% you really need, and delete the rest. Now, you may want to keep an email for a few days until you delete it. This is where the 'halfway to the bin' can be very useful.

For example, you receive an invitation to a conference. You put all the relevant information in your calendar. However you may want to keep the invitation handy until the conference is over. The folder 'halfway to the bin' is a good place to do so.

A simple trick to regularly purge your 'halfway to the bin' folder: whenever you put a new email in it, have a quick look at the emails already in it and delete the ones which can be deleted.

Ordering folders

The main reason I suggest to number your folders from one to nine is to simplify the next step, the purge and prune of your emails. By creating empty folders and numbering them in order, these new folders will automatically come on top of all your existing folders. This will make the next step easier, as I will explain a bit further.

Personal and archive

I suggest having a separate folder for your personal emails. I also suggest creating, if need, be a folder called 'archive'. You can decide to archive old emails either per dates or per previous jobs.

STEP TWO: PURGE AND PRUNE

You are now ready for the fun part, the purge and prune. As mentioned above, you need to be ruthless with what you keep and what you delete. Only keep what you must keep. Remember the simple questions to ask yourself when reviewing emails and deciding what to keep or not:

- **Be honest**   Will I need it?
- **Be ruthless**   When was the last time I used it?
                      What is the worst thing which can happen if I throw it?
- **Be smart**   Can I find it easily somewhere else?

I remember working with a lady in Perth, Australia. She had kept many emails over the years. Going through this process was liberating for her. In a few hours she deleted about 20,000 emails. More importantly, she set up a filing system which worked very well for her, whereas before she was wasting a lot of time searching for emails.

You have now your new filing structure on top of your folders, and all your existing folders below. You filing structure should look like this:

Folders
01. halfway to the bin
02. strategy
03. marketing
04. sales
05. finance
06. delivery/production
07. administration
08. personal
09. archive
Administration templates

Clients
Events
Finance
Interesting articles
Legal
Offsite
Prospects
Recruitment
Strategy
etc …

The folders labelled 01 to 09 are empty. The others are your existing ones, full of emails. Take the first one — in this example 'administration templates' — and review. The amount of time you need to spend purging and pruning this folder depends how important it is for you to have an efficient 'administration' folder. If you don't use this folder much, have a quick look and quickly delete some emails or move the whole folder to '09 Archive'. If it's worth your time, review each emails and decide which ones to delete.

Once done, rename the folder appropriately and move it into your new structure. In this example, you might rename this folder 'template' and move it under the folder '07. administration'.

In my experience, this is the quickest way to do an efficient purge and prune of your emails.

After all this, do you really need a filing structure?

I have always found it quite inefficient to have to manage two soft filing systems, one for all documents such as Word®, Excel® and PowerPoint®, and one for emails. After all, emails are just another type of document.

Let's say you have a folder in your personal drive called 'Nestle'. You would not create three sub-folders 'Nestle Word', 'Nestle Excel' and 'Nestle PPt'. You would put all your Word, Excel and PowerPoint documents in one folder 'Nestle'. Why do we have to make an exception for emails?

It is actually very easy to file an email in your personal drive or storage area. Just have the two windows side by side, the Outlook windows and the personal drive windows, and drag an email into your personal drive. As simple as that.

Now, I am being pretty extreme there, and for most people it is worth having these two systems, either because they need to keep many emails or because they have so many already that it would take too much time to completely reorganise their soft filing system.

However, this is a good trick to know as you might want to file some emails in either your personal drive or a shared drive. For example, you might want to keep an email because it could be of use to the whole team. The shared drive would be a perfect place for this. By dragging and dropping this email into the shared drive windows, you have now filed this email in the shared drive and everyone can open and read it.

3.3 CALENDAR & TASK – THERE IS A LIFE BEYOND INBOX

Most people use Outlook as an email receiving system. When in Outlook, most of their time is spent checking emails in their inbox. They use their calendar to record meetings with other people and rarely, if ever, use Task and Notes.

Outlook is much more than an email management tool. Above all, it should be your time and task management tool. As mentioned earlier, if you want to be effective, you need to have very strong control of how you spend your time. I should be able to ask you how you spent your time by bunches of fifteen minutes on Wednesday three weeks ago. If you can't answer this question, you can probably improve your effectiveness.

Outlook is a great efficiency and effectiveness tool. It can help you organise your tasks and key priorities, and to manage your time more effectively.

Let's step away from Outlook for a second and discuss task management. When coaching people at their desk, I ask them how they manage their priorities on a daily basis. The most common answer I get is what I call the 'note pad to do list'. At the start of every day, the person takes his or her note pad and writes down what he or she has to do for the day. It looks like this:

Monday — 'to do' list
– call Sophie regarding proposal
– prepare strategy session
– read market overview
– client & prospects calls
– call Eva regarding marketing launch
– prepare marketing meeting
– David on leave
– call Antoine to organise tennis this week
– prepare document for executive meeting
– respond to tender from ABC
– etc …

Figure 3.2: Standard 'to-do' list

On the one hand they like their 'to do' list. It enables them to keep track of all that needs to be done. They can tick things off as they go, which is quite satisfying. However they are often quite frustrated as things keep being added to their lists during the day. At the end of the day, half of what they wanted to do is not done.

Let's review the list above to understand how much time you need to spend on each task.

Monday — 'to do' list	
Task	time needed
– call Sophie regarding proposal	5 min
– prepare strategy session	3 hr
– read market overview	5 min
– client & prospects calls	1 hr 30 min
– call Eva regarding marketing launch	5 min
– prepare marketing meeting	1 hr
– David on leave	
– call Antoine to organise tennis this week	5 min
– prepare document for executive meeting	2 hr
– respond to render from ABC	2 hr
– etc …	
total needed	10 hr

Figure 3.3: 'To do' list with allocated time

The key thing is to make a distinction between the time-consuming tasks and the quick ones. The quick ones should not be in your 'to do' list, but in your Outlook Task. The time-consuming one should not be in your 'to do' list, but in your Outlook Calendar.

Monday — 'to do' list		
Task	time needed	in Outlook
– call Sophie regarding proposal	5 min	Task
– prepare strategy session	3 hr	Calendar
– read market overview	5 min	Task
– client & prospects calls	1 hr 30 min	Calendar
– call Eva regarding marketing launch	5 min	Task
– prepare marketing meeting	1 hr	Calendar
– David on leave		Reminder
– call Antoine to organise tennis this week	5 min	Task
– prepare document for executive meeting	2 hr	Calendar
– respond to render from ABC	2 hr	Calendar
– etc …		
total needed	10 hr	

Figure 3.4: 'To do' list including time required and where noted

In the example above, there was no indication in the first list of how much time was needed for each task, when was a good time to do it, and if the person could realistically achieve all this on the day.

The person might already have quite a few meetings and only have four hours available. In the example they need about ten hours to get everything done, and this is without allowing any time for interruptions or any crises. In reality the person probably needs twelve to thirteen hours to get all this done.

And we wonder why we end up stressed at the end of most days and frustrated we have not achieved all we wanted to.

The rule is simple but very important. Whatever is time consuming should not be in a daily 'to do' list but in your calendar. You can either put it straight away in your calendar or write it in your weekly plan and decide weekly when to do it. We will discuss in the next chapter the concept of 'weekly plan'.

For quick tasks, you can use a 'short task' list. However I personally recommend using Outlook Task. With Outlook Task you can allocate a specific date for the task to be done and forget about it until then. If you forget to do it on the day, Outlook Task will automatically bring this task back the next day and so on until you delete it. More on Outlook Task at the end of this chapter.

EFFICIENT USE OF OUTLOOK CALENDAR

Your Calendar should be a reflection of how you spend your time.

If you want to be effective, you need to have a very good command of how you spend your time. Your Calendar should be your time management tool, used to record how you spend your time. As mentioned before: 'What gets measured gets managed'. You need to use your calendar to measure and record how you spend your time.

This is true wether you are using an electronic diary, such as Outlook, or a paper one. I am not hung up about Outlook Calendar. I have met people using a paper calendar very efficiently and others using their Outlook Calendar very poorly. However Outlook Calendar is great to use as you can synchronise with devices such as BlackBerry®, iPhone® or smartphone. You can drag and drop emails into it and it is very visual and easy to use.

Use your calendar for any time-consuming meetings with others and self

Too often we use our calendar only to book meetings with other people. As importantly, you should book meetings with yourself and respect these booked meetings.

It always surprises me how we lack respect for our own time. If you have an important meeting with someone in your diary, you would plan to arrive on time. I would be surprised if during the meeting you made a few phone calls, allowed a few interruptions to answer questions from colleagues, and checked your emails. Of course you would not.

Why then do we do it when we have a meeting with ourselves? We might have blocked time to work on something very important, something which will have a high impact on our performance. Why do we allow ourself to start late, to be interrupted by colleagues, to check a few unrelated emails while working on this project and so on?

If you have a meeting with yourself on something important, you should treat this meeting as if it was a meeting with a very important client. You may want to isolate yourself to avoid interruptions from colleagues and temptations from yourself to do other things. For example you may want to work from home or in a meeting room from time to time, to be concentrated on your work without interruptions and distractions.

The start of this is to book meetings with yourself in your Calendar, and to respect these meetings.

Let me breathe

I have seen two extreme ways to manage Calendar. Most people have what I call the 'empty calendar'. Their calendar is only used to record meetings with other people. They do not plan their day and do not block time with themselves to work on important issues.

Most of the time their diary often looks quite empty, with only a few appointments in it. On a specific day, they might have many tasks and projects they need to work on, however it does not show in their calendar.

As a result they look quite available for meetings. And they are often complaining they never have enough time to do all they have to do.

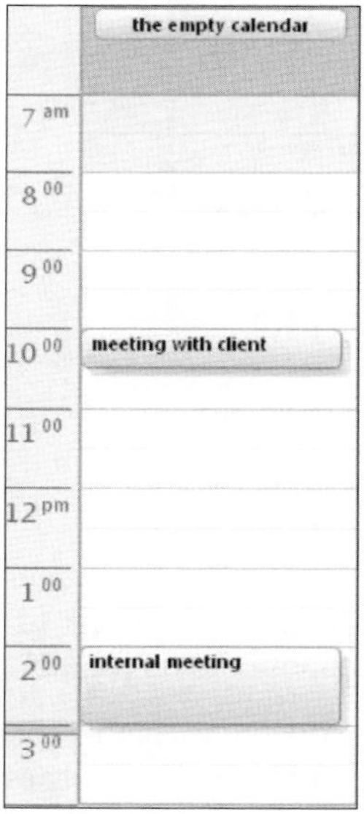

Figure 3.5: The empty calendar

Other people have a 'crazy calendar'. Their calendar is full of back-to-back meetings, most of them with other people, and a few desperate attempts to block time for themselves.

They are often rushing from one meeting to another, and as soon as one meeting finishes later than expected, they are late to the next one. They have little time to do all the tasks they are supposed to do. They are struggling to return phone calls and emails. The time they have blocked with themselves to work on specific project often ends up being taken by urgent meetings or to manage a few unexpected urgent crises. They finish most days exhausted after this race between meetings, and frustrated as they do not have enough time to work on long-term projects.

	the empty calendar		the crazy calendar
9 am			team meeting
10 00	meeting with client		1.1 with John
11 00			marketing steering committee
12 pm			
1 00			lunch with client
2 00	internal meeting		performance review with Steve
3 00			
4 00			meeting with Mike to prepare offsite
5 00			prepare proposal for client

Figure 3.6: The crazy calendar

I'm reminded of the senior executive showing me his diary with back-to-back meetings all day and asking me, 'When am I supposed to do my job?'

When people end up taking work home and working evenings and weekends, their performance is reduced. They struggle to meet deadlines and to spend enough time on the long-term, critical projects. Worse, it has an impact upon their personal life. Stress increases and time spent with loved ones is reduced.

You might think I exaggerate there, but I have seen many of these frantically busy managers.

I suggest a more efficient way of planning your schedule, something I call 'let me breathe'.

First, use your calendar to block time both for meetings with others and for meetings with yourself. Your calendar is your tool to decide how to effectively plan time. It should reflect precisely how you spend your time.

Secondly, leave 'breathing space' in your calendar between meetings. You should leave your calendar 'breathing', otherwise you will suffocate.

Breathing time is not thinking time. If you need time to think about a specific project, book a meeting with yourself to do so. Breathing time in between meetings will allow you to:

- have some flexibility if you need a little bit more time at the end of a meeting;
- have the time to debrief the meeting back at your desk rather than running straight away to the next one;
- take action on a few quick tasks, such as returning some calls;
- prepare for the next meeting.

	the empty calendar	let me breathe	the crazy calendar
9 am		prepare document for executive committee	team meeting
			1.1 with John
10 00	meeting with client		marketing steering committee
11 00		marketing steering committee	
12 pm		lunch	
1 00		1.1 with John	lunch with client
2 00	internal meeting	prepare proposal for client	performance review with Steve
3 00			
4 00			meeting with Mike to prepare offsite
5 00			prepare proposal for client

Figure 3.7: Comparing calendar styles

However well organised we are, we all need time for interruptions, crises and to do the little things such as returning phone calls and responding to emails. How much time you need per day will depend on your role and your personality.

Someone in a reactive role, such as a PA or an admin person, might only block a few meetings per day and have a lot of open space in between. An executive might have a calendar full of meetings (with other people and also with him or herself) and only leave 30 minutes' breathing time in between.

I do not pretend to solve the frantic path of the people described above just with this trick. In a sense this is the purpose of this entire book. But keep in mind that if your calendar is either empty or crazy, it is probably a good indication that you can improve your efficiency and effectiveness.

Let me breathe to re-energise

Over years I have also started recognising another key value of this 'breathing time'. It enables people to re-energise, to recharge their mental battery.

In the early 1950s, researchers Eugene Aserinsky and Nathan Kleitman discovered that during both nights and days, we are going through 90 to 120-minute cycles. To be on top of our performance during the day, every 90 to 120 minutes, we need a period of rest and recovery.

After 90 to 120 minutes spent concentrating, both our energy level and level of concentration drops down. We start yawning, we need to stretch and to move. We can fight against it by flooding our body with stress hormones and continuing to maintain concentration. This works short term but the long-term physical cost is a build up of toxins in our body.

To stay highly productive during the day, it is imperative to 'breathe' and relax regularly. You will struggle to be concentrating well and to stay on top of your performance if you work ten hours straight. You need to take breaks and recharge your mental batteries. Get up from your desk and go for a walk. Get out of the office to get some fresh air and some natural light. Do whatever has a relaxing effect on you.

Several years ago the *Fast Company* business magazine asked successful professionals how to avoid being burnt out. Nearly all of them explained how they have put in place daily routines to regularly renew themselves.

A FEW USEFUL TIPS ON OUTLOOK CALENDAR

Use the appropriate view

Outlook Calendar enables you to choose a view per day, work week, week or month. I personally prefer the 'Work Week' view as it enables me to see my whole week and to see visually the time taken by each activity.

The difference between the 'Work Week' view and the 'Week' view is that in the 'Work Week' view you can visually see the time taken by each activity, whereas in the 'Week' view each activity is just a line, whether it's a five-minute one or an activity that requires three hours.

You can decide which days you want to include in your 'Work Week' by clicking on Tools/Options then clicking on 'Calendar Options' in the Preference tab and selecting the days of your work week. For most people the days selected will be Monday to Friday.

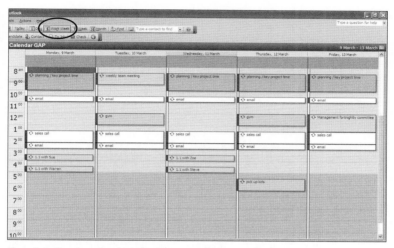

Figure 3.8: Choosing a 'work week' view

Drag and drop emails

As noted earlier, one of the great functions of Outlook is the possibility to drag and drop emails into Calendar or Task.

Let's say you receive an email which will require one hour of your time to deal with. Rather than procrastinating and saying to yourself, 'I need to do this but don't have one hour now, I'll come back to this later,' you should open your Calendar and decide when you will do it.

You can then drag and drop the email into your Calendar as shown below. This will open a Calendar entry, and you just have to choose the date and time. Remember that dragging an email into Calendar will only copy the content of the email. It will not drag attachments. It will not move the email; only copy it into Calendar. Your email will still be in your inbox and so you need to either delete or file it.

If you need to drag an attachment, you can click on the 'Move to Folder' icon and choose 'Calendar' as shown below. This will move both the content of the email and the documents attached into a Calendar entry. It will not copy your email but move it. Your email will no longer be in your inbox.

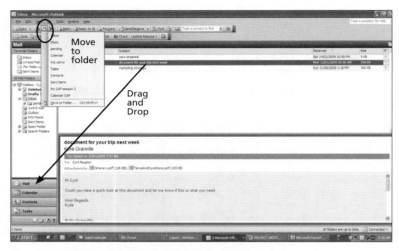

Figure 3.9: 'Dragging and dropping' emails in Outlook

Recurrent appointments

You might need to set some recurring appointments in your Calendar. For example, if you are part of a weekly meeting, you can set a recurrent appointment every week on the same date and time. You can also set recurrent appointments with yourself. You might decide you want to keep every morning from 8:00 am 'til 10:00 am for yourself to work on key projects. You can set a recurrent appointment every week day from 8:00 am until 10:00 am.

Simply create a new appointment and click on the 'Recurrence' icon. Then select the recurrent features and save.

We use a lot recurrent meetings with the people we coach. In the chapter on personal leadership we discuss the concept of the effective week. Once you have worked out on paper what your effective week will look like, you will need to implement many recurrent meetings in your diary. This will enable you to have enough time for key projects. The 'other stuff' will have to fit around those, and not the contrary.

Colour code your meetings

You have the possibility in Outlook to colour code your appointments. It's a great feature and I strongly encourage you to use it. It will liven up your Calendar and make it more user-friendly. More importantly, it will enable you to have a simple and easy way to see how you spend your time.

First you need to segment your time into four or five categories. Then you need to choose a colour per category. For example:

- Creativity/planning/long-term project   green
- Internal meetings   grey
- Business development meetings   yellow
- Personal time   blue

To colour code your appointments you need first to create the above categories and then categorise each appointment accordingly.

If you are using Outlook 2003, right click on any appointment and select 'Label'. Then select 'Edit Labels' and write down your categories in front of the colour selected. You can then right click on an appointment you want to colour, select 'Label' and choose the right category.

If you are using Outlook 2007 or 2010, right click on any appointment and select 'Categorize'. Then select 'All Categories' and write down your categories in front of the colour selected. You can then right click on an appointment you want to colour, select 'Categorize' and choose the right category.

EFFICIENT USE OF OUTLOOK TASK

Use Outlook Task as a reminder for five-minute tasks

I am always amazed to see how much stress can be created by the one million things we have to do and that accumulate in our subconscious. As mentioned previously, I have found that stress is not linked to the amount of work we have. Stress is linked to the way we manage it.

I often see people completely overwhelmed with the amount of work they have to do. In reality they stress not because of the amount of work they have, but because they have no idea how they will achieve it. Their conscious and subconscious is full of unattended tasks. They know they have to do them, but don't know when and if they will even to get to them.

Once you have reviewed all your priorities for the week, decided what you will do and, as importantly, what you will not do, and then allocated time for your key projects in your calendar, you will feel far more in control and experience far less stress. We will discuss this in detail in chapter four.

Use Outlook as you time and task management tool. For time-consuming meetings with others or yourself, use Outlook Calendar. For quick and short tasks, use Outlook Task.

Outlook Task will enable you to fight against distraction. When you think about a short task you need to do, capture it in Task. Write what you have to do, and when it needs to be done.

As mentioned with Outlook Calendar, Outlook Task is just a tool. If you prefer using a paper task list, that's fine. However I find Outlook Task very convenient to use. You can drag and drop emails into Tasks. You can allocate each task to a specific day. If you forget to do a task on a day, it is automatically carried over for the next day.

So whether you use Outlook Task or have a paper document for your tasks is not the key point. They key point here is to use Outlook Calendar for your time-consuming activities and Outlook Task or your task list for all your quick tasks.

If you only have a few tasks per day, put a reminder and allocate in breathing time.

If you only have a few short tasks per day, the easiest way to handle them is to create an Outlook Task for each, to allocate the appropriate date and to tick the reminder box.

When you create a new task, only choose the 'Start date'. Outlook will automatically allocate the same 'Due date'. As I only suggest using Outlook Task for short tasks, it does make sense to have the same 'Start' and 'Due' date.

When ticking the reminder box, it will automatically set the reminder on the 'Start date' previously selected. As for the time of the reminder, I suggest choosing the default one early in the morning. You can set the default time for all your tasks by going into Tools/Options and choosing the 'Reminder Time' under Task.

Only put a specific time for a Task if there is a specific reason why you should do this task at this particular time. Otherwise set the default time for Task as early morning, for example at 7:00 am. When you open the computer in the morning, Outlook will open a 'Reminder Window' listing your tasks.

Do not action these straight away. I suggest actioning your tasks during your breathing time. As explained earlier, your Calendar should be full of meetings with others and yourself, but with gaps between each meeting, what I call your breathing time. This is the perfect time to action all your short tasks.

If you have many short tasks per day, group them

Once you get into the habit of using Outlook Task, you might get to a point where you have many small tasks to do each day and you are starting to struggle to do them all. Or you might be in a job which requires you to do many small tasks every day.

A typical example is a sales person. He might have to do many calls every day: prospecting new clients, following up on proposals, organising meetings with existing clients and so on. Each call can be considered as a five-minute task. However if the sales person has twenty calls to make every day, he will struggle to have them done only in breathing time.

In this case I suggest grouping and batching these sales call tasks. For example, the sales person might decide he should dedicate one hour per day for all his sales phone calls. He should set up a one hour meeting with himself in his Calendar every day to do his phone calls. He should also record each phone call as a task and create a category in Task called 'sales call'.

When the time has come in his Calendar to do his phone calls, all the sales person has to do is to go into Outlook Task, arrange the view by categories, go into the category called 'sales call' and do the phone calls scheduled for that day.

To create a category in Outlook, simply create a new task or open an existing one and click on 'Categories'. If you are using Outlook 2003, select 'Master Category List' or, if you are using Outlook 2007, click on 'All Categories'. You can then create the category you need, for example 'sales call'. Next time you create a task, you can select this category by clicking on 'Categories'.

There are many scenarios where batching tasks can be useful. For example someone with accounting responsibilities might have many small entries to make. Or someone with administrative responsibilities might have many small database entries to make.

3.4 OUTLOOK – FROM TRICKS TO HABITS

The point of this chapter on Outlook has not been to transform you into an IT Outlook guru. There are so many more things Outlook can do. My job is to show how Outlook can become a great efficiency and effectiveness tool. If you want to be effective, you need a great task and time management tool. Outlook can be this tool.

Now reading this chapter is one thing, putting it into practice is another. I suggest spending some time now reviewing this chapter, and deciding what could be useful to you. Answer the two following questions:

How can I become more efficient in using Outlook?

What do I need to practise?

Once you are clear on how you can improve, open your Outlook and play with it. Try what I have suggested, see how this would work for you and practise it for a while.

PERSONAL LEADERSHIP: THE TRUE MIND-SHIFT TO PERFORMANCE

PART TWO

4

" The efficiency and effectiveness journey was literally life changing on both a personal and professional level. I now feel confident that I am on top of all my day to day tasks and spend the majority of my time focused on the projects that will have the most impact on the success of my organisation.

Manager, Marketing & Communications
NGS Super

Chapter 4

THE SIMPLE STEPS OF EFFECTIVENESS

Efficiency versus effectiveness

So far we have focused mainly on efficiency in work habits. As mentioned at the start of this book, there are two critical skills which impact personal performance: efficiency and effectiveness.

Efficiency habits are linked to 'how' we do things. Efficiency is defined by 'doing the things right'. Applied to our work environment, this means being efficient with our hard and soft files, being aware of and fighting against time wasters and having a system to efficiently manage tasks and time.

Effectiveness habits are different. Personal effectiveness or personal leadership is linked to the 'what' you are doing. Are you focusing on the few things which are critical to your performance? Are you doing the *right* things?

In this section of the book we will focus on the effectiveness/personal leadership work habits.

After all we have gone through in this book, and I hope what we covered has been of benefit to you, this might come as a surprise: becoming more efficient is easy.

When I coach people, I am aware of the visible and invisible problems. The efficiency issues are visible and screaming loud and clear: messy desks, unread emails, long 'to do' lists … people sweat hard when I work with them on fixing these, but they see the impact quickly. They suddenly realise how great it is to be more organised, to be on top of their emails and their tasks.

The effectiveness issues are less visible and more difficult to change. One of the biggest effectiveness issues is that most people are reacting to the day-to-day crises rather than focusing on a few important activities. They are addicted to the buzz of our modern office life with their emails, BlackBerry®, interruptions, and so on. They fail to recognize the impact it has on their performance and their level of stress.

And like any drug addict, recognizing the problem is the first step to fixing it. Once they agree there is a better way, fighting against their old habits is as hard as it would be for anyone who has tried to stop drinking or smoking would know.

A constant drag into reactive mode

We are constantly pushed in our everyday life towards reacting rather than acting. More and more people work in open plan offices, where it is hard to avoid interruptions and distractions. We rush from one urgent meeting to another and have to deal with many crises every day.

Even the wonderful tools and technology we are using are creating stress and a reactive approach. We couldn't live without our BlackBerry®, iPhone® or similar device. We have Outlook or something like it constantly open. We are in a world of constant communications.

We are expected to be 'on call' during our working hours and often outside them. I often hear people mentioning that if they don't check and respond to emails constantly, someone will call them within an hour of sending an email to them to ask why they haven't yet responded.

There is, in my opinion, a strong misunderstanding of 'performance'. Too often we link performance to one's ability to react instantly. If someone reacts very quickly, seems very busy and runs a hundred miles an hour every day, they must be working hard and well.

I believe this is dangerous and misleading. Performance is not defined by the number of things you do or by the hours you work. I have met people who are working twelve hours a day but fail to perform and others working nine to five in the same job and being high performers. I remember the manager of a team of financial planners who mentioned that his best-performing planner was only working six hours a day whereas some of the low performing ones were working at least nine to ten hours per day.

Performance is primarily linked to what you are focusing on, not how quickly you are getting it done.

If you live in Sydney and want to go to Newcastle (north of Sydney), taking a Ferrari and driving south towards Wollongong (south of Sydney) will get you quickly in the wrong place. You would be better off taking a bike and riding towards Newcastle.

Sun Tzu, a Chinese general and philosopher from the 6th century BC, wrote an interesting book, *The Art of War*. One of his quotes is so relevant even today:

> **'Strategy without tactics is the slowest route to victory.**
> **Tactics without strategy is the noise before defeat.'**

Let me explain this in the context of performance.

'Strategy without tactics is the slowest route to victory.' If you know what is truly important to your success and performance and you focus on it, even if you are disorganised, even if your desk is messy, your emails are out of control, you will perform. You will, little by little, move towards your goals. You will pay a price for your lack of efficiency — it will take you more time than needed and you will probably feel pretty stressed along the way, but you will get there.

'Tactics without strategy is the noise before defeat'. You can be super organised and efficient, your desk tidy and all your documents in the right place and easily accessed, your inbox in control and your day very organised. Yet if you do not focus on the few things which are key to your performance, you are unlikely to be successful.

However, the journey to move from working reactively to proactively is not easy. It requires a real mind shift: from reacting to all the day-to-day issues to being a leader who decides what to focus on and makes it a priority beyond all the small interruptions.

I am not a manager. Why should I be a leader?

When I use the word 'leader' and 'leadership skills', I do not use them in the sense of managing and leading people. Each of us, in whatever role we are in, has a choice to be a reactive follower or a proactive leader. We can let the day-to-day issues rule our days, or we can be proactive and decide what we will and will not focus on.

You can be in a very reactive job, such as working in a call centre or managing the administrative tasks for a team, and still be a proactive leader. For example, an administrative person can view their job as purely reacting to others' requests, or they can decide there is a proactive component to their role. They can take some initiative and suggest some changes to processes which will make a big difference to everyone. They can then decide to help each member of the team to understand this new process and 'coach' them in this area.

Proactive behaviour is not attached to a role. It is a personal decision.

Aligning your day to day actions with your long term goals

Ideally, to be effective and perform at work, each person in the company needs to align their day-to-day activities with the strategy and goals of their company.

In an ideal corporate world, the high-level strategy is translated into divisional goals for each division. Each division then translates these goals into a Personal Plan or KPI (Key Performance Indicators) for each person. The aim is to clarify for each employee their key projects and key activities for the year. You could be involved with specific key projects and also with key ongoing activities such as regularly calling and meeting clients and prospects for sales people.

In theory their KPI should motivate what each person is doing on a day-to-day basis, how they daily focus their time and effort.

This is often called the corporate cascade, as it is supposed to flow from the top-level strategy through to what people are doing on a day-to-day basis.

Figure 4.1: The 'corporate cascade'

The reality is somewhat different. Between the high-level goals and what people are doing on a day-to-day basis, there is often a gap. According to recent studies, two-thirds of corporate strategy is never executed. There is a real gap between company strategies, divisional goals, KPIs and what executives, senior managers and teams do on a day-to-day basis.

Companies spend a lot of effort and resources in developing their strategy. They either work with external consulting firms such as McKinsey, Bain or BCG to develop their long-term strategy, or the leadership team undertake a number of in-depth offsite meetings throughout the year.

Amazingly, two-thirds of the decisions from these 'think tanks' are never executed. The issue is often not on the quality of the strategy and action plan decided; it is how well these plans are turned into actions by all.

People are working hard but not always working smart. There is often a misalignment between what they are supposed to do, what will have a long-term high impact on the performance of their company, and what they are doing each day.

The focus of this section of the book is to close this gap between your daily activities and what you MUST be doing to perform.

'Execution' and 'Alignment' are two key words which summarise this approach.

Figure 4.2: Executing and aligning the 'corporate cascade'

In my experience, effectiveness at work comes down to four simple steps. Follow these simple steps, and you will achieve what you are aiming for:

1. Think quarterly: be clear on your goals and high-impact activities
2. Plan weekly: make them a must
3. Act daily: take action regardless
4. Review and change if necessary.

■ Think quarterly: be clear on your goals and high-impact activities

Effective people first know what they want to achieve; what goals they want to reach. If you are running a marathon and you are not clear on what success means for you, how can you be successful? You could finish last and be successful if your goal was to finish the marathon, or you could finish second and fail if your goal was to win.

Being clear on your goals, and therefore on which high-impact activities are necessary to reach these goals, is critical to your success and performance.

It is very hard to make the link at an individual level between the yearly strategy of your company and what you need to do on a daily basis. I have found that successful teams clarify on a quarterly basis what they want to achieve for the next quarter and how this will affect each member of the team. They do not only think yearly, they consider their strategy and goals at least on a quarterly basis.

This is not a new idea. In 1937 Napoleon Hill published a great book called *Think and Grow Rich*. It has sold millions of copies around the world and is still printed and sold today.

Hill explained how he was asked by Andrew Carnegie, the famous Scottish-American entrepreneur often regarded as the second richest man in history, to interview highly successful people to find out if there was a common trait that made them successful. Napoleon Hill discovered that one the key characteristic of such people is that they are very clear on their goals; on what they want to achieve. They have a strong desire to achieve to the point they have written clearly their long-term goals and review them daily.

■ Plan weekly: make them a must

Once you are clear on your goals and on the few activities which will help you to reach them, you need to make these high-impact activities a must. These activities should not fall under the 'I will when I have time' or 'I should'. They need to be 'I must and I am taking massive actions today'.

How many times have you heard someone saying 'I should exercise' or 'I should eat healthier food', only to see little change happening?

I would like to share a personal example which illustrates this shift from 'I should' to 'I must.' I remember someone in our neighbourhood who was extremely overweight and looked very unhealthy. I did not know him personally but most people in our area had seen him around. You couldn't help noticing him.

Then something changed. Over the course of a year and a half, he started losing a dramatic amount of weight. We saw him walking every day and, in the end, jogging and cycling.

One day a friend of my wife stopped him. She had never spoken to him before and apologised for being curious, but could not help asking what had happened, what triggered this amazing change.

And he kindly explained his story. He had been overweight for a long time and had been thinking for many years 'I should do something about it'. Then one day, in his early thirties, he went to see a new doctor who was straightforward with him. After doing a series of health tests, he was told by his doctor that if he did not change his way of living he only had a few years to live.

This was a shock for him. Improving his health suddenly became an 'I must', not an 'I should'. Once this mental shift was made, the rest was relatively easy. He began walking every day and paying attention to his diet. After a year and a half he had lost most of his excess weight and was feeling 100% better.

He made his health a 'must' and took massive actions.

Effective people are really strong at this. They know what their goals are and are really good at making them a 'must'.

In this chapter, we will review how to implement 'an effective week' in your diary. We will discuss how to plan weekly to ensure the right amount of focus and time spent on high impact activities.

▪ Act daily: take actions regardless

You need to spend most of your time and energy on these high-impact activities. It is so easy to be distracted on a daily basis by a hundred little things. We are constantly bombarded by emails, often when away from our desk, through our BlackBerry® or iPhone®. In the office we are interrupted, on average, every three minutes. Most of us can't even go back home and switch off from work — we have many ideas and thoughts running through the back of our mind.

You might have planned your high-impact activities in your diary. It will take courage — I call this personal leadership — to act on them on a daily basis. You need to act on your high-impact activities regardless of all the noise around you.

On a daily basis you should neither think long term nor plan. This should be done quarterly and weekly. On a daily basis you are just acting as previously decided and planned. You are just taking massive actions to progress towards your long-term goals.

■ Review and change if necessary

Success is also linked to the ability to constantly review what has been achieved, what has worked and not worked, and to change direction if necessary in order to achieve your goals.

Successful people are stubborn. They know what they want to achieve and are prepared to take massive actions to reach their goals. They also regularly review what they are doing to reach these goals and are prepared to change their actions if necessary.

Moving towards a goal is a bit like driving a sailboat towards a specific point. It is unlikely you will be able to go straight to your final direction. You will need to often review your position and change your direction. And it's the same for moving toward your goals.

One of the most amazing examples of persistence and adaptation toward a goal is the story of Thomas Edison. He was clear on his goal — to invent the electric light bulb — and made many attempts to reach it. He tried many times and failed many times.

The story says that when he reached experiment 9,999 and failed, he was asked by a reporter, 'Sir, are you going to fail 10,000 times?' Edison confidently replied, 'I have not failed at each attempt; rather I have succeeded at discovering another way not to invent an electric lamp.'

He was very clear about his goal and every attempt was one step towards it. He was ready to review his approach after each attempt, and change accordingly, to move towards his goal.

5

" It went much further than simply time management by addressing the core issue – how to ensure that what you do on a day-to-day basis is aligned with your KPIs, your departmental objectives and your overall corporate vision.

Communications Manager
Asgard Wealth Solutions

Chapter 5

THINK QUARTERLY: BE CLEAR ON YOUR GOALS AND HIGH-IMPACT ACTIVITIES

5.1 A MIND SHIFT FROM REACTIVE FOLLOWER TO PROACTIVE LEADER

How we prioritise

People often confuse 'deadline' and 'value'. When I coach people, they are struggling with long 'to do' lists. They end up stressed because many things on their list don't get done and new tasks are constantly added. At the end of the day they are quite frustrated as most of their 'big-ticket items' are repeatedly put on the back burner due to the daily crises.

I often ask people how they prioritise, how they choose every day what they will do, what they will start with. The answers vary from 'What is most urgent,' to 'What is the most important,' or 'Who asked for it,' or even 'What I enjoy doing.'

The most common answer I get is 'due date' or 'deadline'. If they have two tasks to do, one due today and one due in two weeks, they will start with the one due today. The second most common answers I hear are 'How important the work is' and 'What value it will bring to the organisation.'

But even when someone thinks that they prioritise based on what is more important, they often confuse the words 'urgent' and 'important'. When asked why they chose one task compared to another one, they reply, 'Because this task is more important.' I then ask why it is more important and they answer, 'Because it is due today.' In actual fact, they have confused the words 'important' and 'urgent'.

The reality is that most people and most organisations prioritise their workload based on deadline.

The reactive versus proactive matrix

Let's draw a simple matrix based on these two prioritisation criteria. It has been used in different formats by time management writers such as Stephen Covey in his book titled *First Things First*. It is a simple and very good tool to understand the danger of falling into day-to-day reaction and to move instead into a culture of high performance.

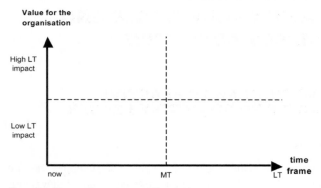

Figure 5.1: The reactive versus proactive matrix

The horizontal axis represents when the work is due, the time frame. When you are working on a task or a project, it could be due now (i.e. today); it could have a middle term deadline or a long-term deadline. Middle and long term will vary depending on your role. If you are in a junior and reactive role, now is now, middle term might be in two weeks and long term might be in one month. If you are the CEO of a large organisation, now is now, middle term might be three months and long term might be two years.

The vertical axis represents what value this work will bring to the organisation. If done well, will this work be of long-term high value for the organisation or not? What will be the impact on the performance of the organisation, on the long-term goals?

It is a very simple and important question to ask yourself constantly when prioritising: what will be the long-term impact of this task on the performance of the business?

In crisis mode

Let's consider the first mode, when we are working on things which are due now or in the short term and that will have a long-term high impact on the performance of your business. This is what I call the crisis mode.

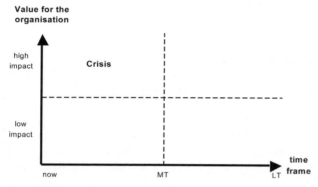

Figure 5.2: The reactive versus proactive matrix — crisis mode

Take a few minutes to think about what you do on a daily basis which fits this category, and to write them down. Think about all the tasks and work you do which are quite urgent and will have an impact on the performance of your business.

Here are the things I hear the most often: urgent client requests, urgent internal requests from senior managers, internal crises between staff members, urgent meetings due to external crises, etc …

I then ask people how they feel if they spend most of their time in crisis mode, if most of their day is spent running from one crisis to another. And the most common answer I get is 'stress, burn out.'

In proactive/personal leadership mode

Let's now consider the second mode, when we are working on things which are not due now. They are not urgent, but we know they will have a high impact on the performance of the business. They are of high value for our organisation. This is what I call the proactive/personal leadership mode.

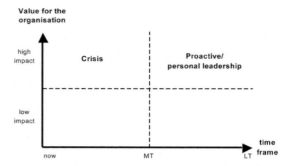

Figure 5.3: The reactive versus proactive matrix — personal leadership mode

Again, take a few minutes to think about the things you do on a daily or weekly basis which fit this category and write them down. Think about all the tasks and work you do which will have a high impact on your business but are not urgent. Whether you do them today or next week will not make a big difference.

Here are some examples of what I hear from people: planning, thinking, creativity, staff development, personal development, process improvement, maintenance, relationship building.

I then ask people how they feel if they spend most of their time in this proactive mode, if most of their day is spent working on non-urgent, high-impact activities. And the most common answer I get is, 'I feel in control.'

In reactive mode

Let's now consider the third mode, when we are working on things which are due now. These are urgent, but we know they will have little or no impact on the performance of the business; they are of low value for our organisation. This is what I call the reactive mode.

Again take a few minutes to think about the things you do on a daily or weekly basis which fit this category and write them down. Think about all the tasks and work you do which are very urgent; they are due soon and someone has asked for them; they have a short deadline. But, if you really think honestly about it, they will have little or no impact on your business. They will make no difference to the performance of the business; they will make no difference in helping to reach the long-term goals.

Some examples of these that I hear from people include: some emails, some meetings, some reporting and dealing with some interruptions.

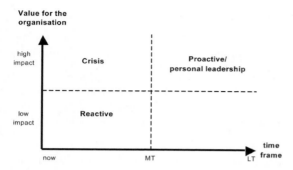

Figure 5.4: The reactive versus proactive matrix — reactive mode

I then ask people how they feel if they spend most of their time in this reactive mode, when most of their day is spent working on urgent low-value activities. And the most common answer I get is 'frustrated'. I often hear people saying they feel empty at the end of the day, knowing they have run fast all day but have not achieved much.

In active disengagement mode

Let's now consider the last mode, when we are working on things that are not due now, are not urgent and will add little or no impact on the performance of the business. These are of low value for our organisation. This is what I call the active disengagement mode.

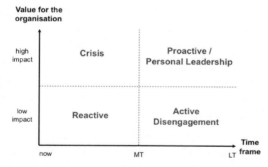

Figure 5.5: The reactive versus proactive matrix — active disengagement mode

Again, take a few minutes to think about what you do on a daily or weekly basis which fits this category and write each down. Think about all the tasks and work you do which are neither urgent nor of value for the organisation.

Examples of active disengagement that I hear include: again some emails, again some interruptions, surfing the internet, playing games, etc ...

From reactive follower to proactive leader

There has been quite a lot of research in this area. When we coach a group of people, we ask them to indicate how they spend their time per mode, and which percent of their time they spend on each mode.

We are also involved in time and motion studies where we interview people to understand how they spend their time and where are the big wasters. As well, shadow some people while they work to record how they spend their time.

What surprises me every time is how little insight people have about how they spend their time. There is always a big difference between asking the question of people and observing them in action. The best way to test this is to ask someone how they spent their time the day before by increments of fifteen minutes. Most people would struggle to answer this question, not to mention asking them how they spent their time the same day a week ago.

I remember asking an executive at the end of a day precisely how he had spent his time in the morning. He could not tell me.

The second interesting fact from our research is to compare high performers with the average worker. When we analyse how people in a team or a division spend their time, we identify a few high performers and compare our findings with the average.

As mentioned above, the results vary, depending upon whether we are asking people or are shadowing them. But an interesting trend always emerges. The figures below are average based on our research. Although each team is quite different, the key message remains the same.

I would like you to try to guess how much time, by percentage, the average office worker spends in each mode. Based on 100%, how much do we spend in crisis mode, in proactive mode, in reactive mode and in active disengagement mode? Make a guess.

Our finding indicates the following: the average office worker spends about 25-30% of their time in crisis mode, 15% of their time in proactive mode, 45-50% of their time in reactive mode and 10% of their time in active disengagement.

The amazing thing is the amount of time spent in reactive mode, on things which are urgent but will have no or little impact on the performance of the business, versus the time spent in proactive mode — only 15% spent on non-urgent activities which will have a high impact on the performance of the business.

With this in mind, try to guess the time spent per mode by high performers.

Our finding indicates the following: high performers spend about 20% of their time in crisis mode, 60% of their time in proactive mode, 15-20% of their time in reactive mode, and 2% of their time in active disengagement mode.

Interesting enough, even high performers spend at least 20% of their time in the crisis mode. Even if you are very effective, crises that you do not control will happen, such as a major problem with one of your clients or a big market change you did not foresee. However, by doing more planning and process improvement, high performers are able to decrease the time they spend in crisis mode.

What is fundamental to understand is the shift from reactive mode to proactive mode. The average office worker spends 30% + 50% = 80% of their time on the left side of the diagram below, on the urgency side.

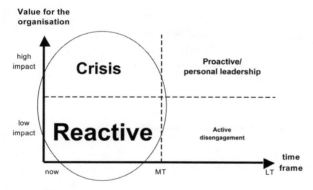

Figure 5.6: How most people spend their time

Most of us prioritise based on deadline before prioritising based on impact. Imagine you have two things to do in front of you. One is due today; someone has requested this urgently. The other task is not urgent at all. You have a few months to do it. Let's be honest, what would most people do?

When I ask this question in my seminar, 99% of people agree they would start with the urgent task due today.

High performers think differently. They ask themselves a key question when prioritising their work: what will be the long-term impact on my performance, on reaching my goals? And if the second, non-urgent task will have a greater impact, they focus on it first. They might manage to spend a little bit of time at the end of the day on the urgent task, but most of their time and energy is focused on activities which will have a long-term impact on their performance.

This is not an easy choice. You will have to resist too many 'urgent' requests. But this is the true mindset of high performers. This is what I call personal leadership.

High performers go this extra mile and ask this key question when prioritising. They have then the courage, if the project due in two months is of higher impact, to focus on it first and do the other one afterwards.

This is the key prioritisation secret of high performers. They start with the high-impact projects first, with the tasks which will be of high value long term for their business, regardless of their urgency.

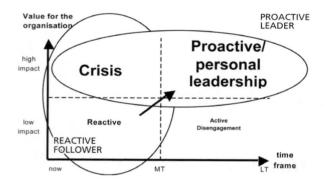

Figure 5.7: How high performers spend their time

This is what I mean by shifting from reactive follower to proactive leader.

General Eisenhower, who later became President of the United States, was known for telling his officers that there is an inverse relationship between urgency and importance: 'Most things which are urgent are not important, and most things which are important are not urgent.'

He told his officers not to bother him with urgent matters. If they focused on urgent issues, he felt they might save a battle but were going to lose the war. He was mainly interested in long-term important discussion. General Eisenhower was not managing the profit and loss of a company, he was managing life and death. And in such a critical area he was convinced of how important it is to focus on high-impact activities rather than urgent ones.

The power of no

It is easy to be a reactive follower, to react to emails, requests, interruptions, crises and so on. All you have to do is sit and wait for things to come to you and react to them. You can fill your whole day with reaction.

It is more difficult to be proactive. It means making choices and decisions based on what you think will have a high impact on the performance of your business. This is why I also call the proactive mode the personal leadership mode. High performers have strong personal leadership skills. They decide what to focus on, rather than allowing other people or day-to-day crises to manage their day.

High performers are not always popular. They often say no to requests and are not the most helpful people. They know their time is limited and of value; they really think about what to allocate it to and, as importantly, what not to spend time on.

To quote the famous effectiveness coach, Peter Drucker: 'The key of strategy is omission.' What is difficult and key is not to decide what you should focus on. When I ask people to list the few projects they should focus on to perform, most people are able to answer this very easily. We all know what we should be doing. What is much more difficult is to say no to the rest. It is critical to decide what you will not do, despite the pressure you might get to do all these other urgent requests.

A favourite mantras of Apple Inc. CEO Steve Jobs is: 'focus means saying no.' This is probably one of the principles which saved Apple from collapse.

Steve Jobs launched Apple Inc. with Steve Wozniack in 1976. They started the business in their parent's garage and build it to a large publicly-listed company. In 1985 Steve was kicked out of Apple for being uncontrollable. When he returned in 1997, Apple was selling so many different products you needed to look at a product chart to decide which products were suited to which clients. To quote Steve, 'What's wrong in this place? It's the products. The products suck!'

Steve Jobs made some tough decisions. He decided what to focus on and what not to focus on. He had to disappoint many people who believed in all the products and features he said no to. But the result was impressive. Apple, on the verge of collapse, came back strongly with the iMac, iTunes, iPhone® and iPad™ to become the biggest IT company in the world.

John Sculley, the Apple CEO from 1983 to 1993 who pushed Steve out in 1985, once wrote: 'What makes Steve's methodology different is that he always believed that the most important decisions you make are not the things that you do but the things you decide not to do.'

It's easy to be reactive. You just have to react to requests, emails and interruptions. It is much harder to be proactive, to decide what to do and what not to do. But this is one of the keys to performance.

A complete shift of mentality

For most people this represents a complete shift of mentality, a new paradigm, from being a reactive follower to a proactive leader. Earlier, I emphasised how hard it is to make that shift.

Being more efficient with your files, emails and managing time wasters is relatively easy. Once you put the effort and start changing your habits, you see the impact immediately. It is easier to locate information; you are starting to be in control of your emails; you are starting to save time by reducing time wasters. You feel great ...

Becoming more effective by shifting from reactive follower to proactive leader is much harder. If you start today spending much more time on high-impact activities, you will not see the difference tomorrow, or the day after. It will probably take a few months to see the impact. And in the meantime you will have to fight hard every day against crises, interruptions and day-to-day reactions. This will be hard.

If you are in sales and you start focusing on your top clients, making more calls, organising more meetings and doing more account planning, it will take a few months before you see the impact on your revenue.

If you are an executive and you decide to spend more time on long-term planning and thinking, on creativity and innovation, on long-term projects, it will take several months — if not more — before you see the impact.

So this shift is very hard to make because the rewards are not instant. But this is where the big rewards are. This is how you can make huge progress in your performance.

If you ask people to spend more time thinking, planning and creating, they would probably say it's a good idea but they never have the time to do so. However one thing successful entrepreneurs, leaders, businessmen and inventors have in common is that they think ahead. They think big; they dream and desire long-term high performance rather than only focus on the day-to-day activities.

One morning, as I was shaving, I was listening to an interview on BBC radio.

Alan Greenspan, ex-Chairman of the US Federal Reserve Bank, was being interviewed regarding a book he published.

Suddenly the journalist asked a surprising question: 'Is it correct that you wrote most of the book in your bath?' I nearly cut myself. And to my surprise Alan Greenspan answered yes: many years ago he had serious back pain and, among other things, his doctor asked him to take an hour's hot bath every day for a month. This was a real constraint for someone as busy as Greenspan but he had no choice. This was for his health. So he did it.

After one month his back had improved but Alan decided to continue the bath routine. He found so much benefit during this hour of non-interrupted thinking time that he continues to allow one hour each day for a hot bath.

If you think you are very busy, imagine the working life of the Chairman of the US Federal Reserve Bank. He was probably one of the busiest people of the finance world, travelling a lot, jumping from one meeting to another one and dealing with key financial issues. And yet he had realised the value of thinking time, the value of non-interrupted time, the value of thinking proactively rather than being reactive all day.

Now I am not suggesting you see your boss to suggest building a bathroom in the middle of the office. I just want to emphasise the importance of focusing regularly on important, non-urgent issues, of thinking ahead and of investing time in being creative.

Personal application — what would work for you?

I would like you to think — and then write — ways you could decrease the time you spend in reactive and crisis modes, and how you can increase the time you spend in proactive mode. Consider how you can plan for and manage the unexpected, and create new habits in the way you use your time.

5.2 THE HIGH PERFORMANCE QUESTION

Think quarterly

I have noted that one of the challenges in many businesses today is the lack of execution and alignment between strategy and what people are doing. Businesses think yearly or sometimes on even larger timeframes. They have an annual or five-year strategy.

However employees have to act accordingly on a daily basis. People struggle to make the link between these yearly goals and what they will do on a day-by-day/hour-by-hour basis. This is, in my experience, one of the biggest problems in performance. The issue is not in strategy and corporate thinking, but in execution.

It is absolutely essential to be clear on your high-impact activities, to be able at any moment to articulate the few things which will have a long-term impact on your performance. The obvious reason is that if you are not clear on what will make you successful, you have little chance to become successful and perform.

This sounds obvious but I am amazed to see how many people work hard without being clear on the few activities which are key for their performance. Successful people are very clear on what they want to achieve and how to get there.

I highly recommend thinking quarterly. Once a quarter, review the yearly plan or strategy or goals and decide what it will mean for you for the next quarter.

Even if your company does not have a well defined strategy and plan, you cannot be effective or be a personal leader if you are not clear on the few things which are key for you and which will make you perform.

The right mindset

I would like you to take 'a proactive mindset'. In deciding what key activities you need to focus on for the next three months, I would like you to move away from deadline-driven projects to impact-driven projects.

I would like you to 'think Pareto'. Vilfredo Pareto was an Italian economist and sociologist. At first he discovered that 80% of land value was owned by 20% of people. The Pareto principle can be applied to many areas. For example in business, often 80% of revenue comes from 20% of clients. Twenty per cent of the total work force of a company produces 80% of the performance. And so on.

The same is true with personal productivity. For most people 80% of their success or performance is produced by 20% of what they do. This means that 80% of what we do only brings very little performance and distract us from the 20% which are vital.

You need to be harsh and avoid wasting time on low-impact activities. Whenever you say yes to something, you are saying no to something else. You need to be very careful on how you commit yourself. What you say yes to could be of low importance, and the time you have invested there is gone forever. Instead you could have spent this time on a high-impact activity which would have had much more impact, in the long term, on your performance.

Too often we confuse performance for quantity. I can work longer hours, do more tasks, have huge 'to do' lists. This is not the point here. You are only thinking quality and scarcity. Take this opportunity once a quarter to move away from the day-to-day madness, to take a good hour, isolate yourself if possible in a place where you can't be interrupted, and think.

The 20% of activities which are key for you do not have to be specific projects. It can also be ongoing activities such as regular phone calls for sales people, regular management and development meetings with their teams for leaders and so on.

I came across a simple but powerful example of the 80/20 rule applied to business. I was reading a comment from a sales person who had 120 corporate customers but realised one day that 95% of his revenue was coming from only five of them. However he was spending 98% of his time on the other clients. This was not leaving him enough time to properly service and grow his top clients.

He took a dramatic decision. He decided to focus on his five top clients and completely stopped contacting the others. In a very short time, his revenue increased dramatically while working fewer hours.

This is not an easy choice. This requires courage and determination. This is the essence of personal leadership. As mentioned earlier, it is easy to be reactive; it is much harder to be proactive. But this is what will lead you to success and performance.

I would like you to take the same mentality, to think about the two or three activities or projects which are key for your performance. I do not want a long 'to do' list, just to identify your real long-term, high-impact activities.

Let's do it: answer the high performance question

Take a pen and paper now. Think about the next three months and answer this question:

What are the two or three projects or activities that if I did extremely well — and nothing else over the next three months — would have a significant impact long-term on my performance and my business?

When answering this question, keep in mind the following:

■ **The two or three projects or activities**

You are not doing your long 'to do' list here. The aim is not to come with a long list of fifty things. I am only interested in the two or three things which are really important, which will make a true impact.

■ **If I did extremely well and nothing else**

You need to take an extreme view in answering this question. Imagine you are facing a life changing event which will seriously impact your time for the next few months. For example, someone very close to you such as one of your children or one of your parents is critically ill.

You decide you want to spend time every day with this person and will only be available at work for a few hours per day. However you want to be as effective as work as before, you do not want your performance in the long term to be affected.

What will you cut and what will you keep doing? What are the few things which are truly important, which will have a real impact on the performance? This is the mentality I am asking you to take for this exercise.

■ **Over the next three months**

Focus only on the next quarter. I want you to think over a period of three months only.

■ **A significant impact long term on my performance**

This should be your main prioritisation mindset. You are not interested in deadlines and what is urgent. Your only focus is on activities which will have a long-term impact on your performance.

With all this in mind, take a few minutes, as long as necessary, and answer this simple question.

Challenge your high-impact activities

This is a critical exercise. The aim is to be clear on the few things which are critical to your performance and then spend most of your time acting on those. It is therefore key to think carefully about which activities you chose to focus on in the next three months.

Once you have written your three high-impact activities, answer this simple question:

If over the next three months I only do these three activities and nothing else, and I do these three activities extremely well, would this be a successful quarter? Would this have a big impact long-term on my performance?

If the answer is yes, then you have your three high-impact activities. If the answer is no, you need to go back to the drawing board and restart the process until you are confident about these three activities.

Room for improvement

Be honest. At the moment, are you spending 60-80% of your time on these three activities?

If you answer yes, well done. You are in the 3% of the population. Continue — you are probably highly effective and are, or will be, highly performing.

If you answer no, don't worry. You are like most people and have room for improvement. Simply follow the steps above and below, and your performance will increase dramatically over the next few months.

It will not be easy. You will have to fight against many distractions, interruptions, crises and other reactive activities which will try to keep you away from your three high-impact activities. You will have to say no to many requests and to people who will want your time for less important, but often more urgent, matters.

General Colin Powell, the US Secretary of State between 2001 and 2005, summarised his view of leadership in 18 leadership lessons. Lesson 1 is so relevant in this context:

> *'Being responsible sometimes means pissing people off:*
> *Good leadership involves responsibility ..., which means that*
> *some people will get angry at your actions and decisions. Trying*
> *to get everyone to like you is a sign of mediocrity.'*

Highly effective people are not always popular because they say no quite often. They are very clear on what they need to focus on and spend little or no time on the rest. And this is not always easy. You need a lot of discipline to fight against daily distractions and interruptions. You need a lot of courage to say no to many low-impact requests, especially when they come from your manager or even higher. This is what true personal leadership is about.

5.3 THE COMPASS PLAN

Once you are clear on your high-impact activities, it is important to write them down in a simple format and keep them front of mind, not once a quarter, but every week and even every day.

I would like to suggest a simple tool I call the compass plan. Now this compass plan is only a tool. You might already use something similar, or you might use and transform the compass plan below. Make it yours, make it a tool you are comfortable working with daily. The important aspect here is not the tool but the thought and action process behind it.

The law of attraction

It is absolutely essential to keep your high-impact activities front of mind. Too many people think about their KPIs (key performance indicators) once a year, write them down and then put them safely in a deep drawer, to be reviewed a year later during their evaluation meeting with their manager.

Once you know what you want to achieve and what are your key impact activities, it gives you an awareness of the opportunities available to get there. Some people call this the law of attraction.

Let's say, for example, that one day you decide to buy a four wheel drive. You never had a four wheel drive before and decide it's now time to purchase one. Suddenly you will start seeing four wheel drives everywhere in the street. Now, there are no more four wheel drives than before; it's just that you are now paying attention.

Another example: you have rented all your life and decide it's now time to buy a house. Suddenly you will start seeing all kinds of information related to buying and financing a house, you will notice all the real estate agents in your area, you will notice all the papers with ads on real estate and so on. Again, the world has not changed — you have.

Being clear on your high-impact activities is very important. It focuses you and your mind on what you want to achieve and the things which are key to get there.

Writing is committing

I believe it is very important to go to the extent of writing your high-impact activities, to take the time to think about what you should focus on for the next few months and put it on paper.

There is a saying in France: 'Ceux que l'on conçoit bien s'annoncent clairement' — what is clear in your mind you can express clearly. Pushing yourself to write it down is a great way to see whether you are really clear about what you need to achieve.

Interesting research in this area was done several years ago. A study of the 1964 graduates of the Harvard University clearly demonstrates the importance to be clear on what you want to achieve. The graduate class of 1964 was asked if they had clear goals. All these high level students responded 'yes'. However when asked how many of them had taken the time to write down their goals, only 5% responded that they had.

The researchers surveyed the same people 20 years later. They wanted to find out whether people had reached their goals. The amazing finding of this survey was that out of the 5% who had written their goals 20 years previously, 95% had achieved them. Out of the 95% who had goals but did not write them down 20 years beforehand, only 5% had achieved them.

The simple fact is that to be so focused and committed on what you want to achieve that you are ready to take a piece of paper and write it down dramatically increases your chance of success.

Take the time once a quarter to write down what you need to focus on for the next three months. It will only take between 30 minutes and an hour, but will greatly increase your focus and chance of performing.

Let's do it

Once you have written down your high-impact activities for the next three months, you should ask yourself a few simple questions for each of them:

- What do I need to focus on in the next three months in relation to these high-impact activities?
- What this will mean on my time each week?
- What measurable outcomes do I want to reach in three months?

You could be working on a very important long-term project which will not be finished in the next three months. During these three months what do you want to focus on? How much time should you realistically dedicate to this? At the end of the three-month period, what milestone do you want to reach? For example, if you are involved in redesigning the website of your company, you could have a goal to have finished the first draft of the content by the end of the three months and to have it approved by the leadership team.

To achieve these milestones, what do you need to do daily or weekly? How do you need to commit your time?

You could be in sales and have decided to increase your sales activity to your top clients over the next three months. You might want to decide to make 15 calls per week to your top clients, have six meetings per week, and get ten proposals in order to generate a revenue of x for the three-month period.

Try to be specific in what you want to achieve. Don't stop at website development or increasing revenue with your key clients. Go to the extent of writing:

High-impact activity	Responsibilities What I need to focus on:	Activity Impact on my time each week:	Success factors Measurable outcomes what do I want to reach:
Website development	▪ feedback/ideas of different stakeholders ▪ build the first draft of the content ▪ source potential suppliers for the design	▪ 1 meeting per week with key stakeholders ▪ 1½ hours of personal thinking time per week ▪ 1 hour fortnightly review with the team	▪ first draft ready and presented to management ▪ first draft of content approved by management
Increase revenue with top clients	▪ more calls to prospects ▪ more meetings with existing & potential large clients ▪ more planning of key opportunities	▪ 15 calls per day = 1 hour per day ▪ 6 meetings per week = 6 x 1½ hrs ▪ 2 x 1 hour account planning sessions per week	▪ 30 new opportunities on the pipeline ▪ $2M additional revenue on pipeline ▪ $1M revenue for 2nd quarter

Figure 5.8: Planning high-impact activities

Regarding your activity, i.e. the impact on your time, you need to be specific and realistic. Do not set yourself for failure if you know it will be impossible to dedicate this amount of time. However you also need to realise that sixty to 80% of your time should to be dedicated to these activities. This might push you to change some of your commitments, to cancel or shorten some of the meetings you are involved in. Being effective is being clear on your high-impact activities and making them a must.

I call this document my compass plan. Other people call it a ninety-day plan. You might already be using a similar document and process. The name of the document and the format does not matter. What is important is to do it once a quarter and even more important what you do with it after. Here are a few suggestions to make the most of your compass plan.

How to make the most of your compass plan

■ Invest the time quarterly

This is a simple process I suggest doing every quarter. It will only take you about one hour. Every three months invest an hour to clarify your high-impact activities and the outcomes expected. The payback for this hour is huge.

■ Use it as a personal leadership tool on a weekly basis

The compass plan is first of all a personal leadership tool. It clarifies for you the high-impact activities you should be focusing on. Do not do it once a quarter and forget it in a deep draw or as a soft document lost somewhere in your computer.

Type it, print it and review it every week. We will discuss later on in this chapter the weekly plan. Once a week you should spend some time planning your next week. Before deciding how you will spend your time next week, read your compass plan, remind yourself of your high-impact activities and with this in mind, plan your week.

■ Ask your manager and your team to challenge your high-impact activities.

Doing your compass plan on your own once a quarter is already a great way to increase your effectiveness. It is also very useful to involve other people in your compass plan. Once you have drafted it, you should discuss it with your manager. It is important you both agree on your high-impact activities.

If you dedicate a lot of time and attention to a project which is not important in the eyes of your manager, this can become a problem for you and your performance.

On the other hand if you have agreed with your manager on what you should be focusing on for the next three months, you have some good arguments if another major project is given to you. You can discuss with your manager which previous key projects should be dumped and replace by the new project.

■ Align your high-impact activities to the team goals

Effective team members are very aware of what the team needs to achieve and how each person will contribute. Another book could be written on this subject, and many very good ones have.

If you are in charge of a team, it is a very important step for the team to go away together for a few hours every quarter to reflect on what was achieved last quarter, where we are at compared to yearly goals and what the team needs to focus on next quarter to succeed. Then translate this into personal plans for the next quarter.

I have seen a few very successful teams. In almost all cases, they have a specific 'goals meeting' once a quarter to discuss what they want to achieve and the high-impact activities to get there. Then each person drafts their own compass plan, based on the team goals discussed, and presents their plan to the team.

Presenting your plan to the team is very important. Ask each member of the team to write a first draft of their compass plan and then to present it to the team.

You want to present your compass plan to the team for a few reasons:

1. You should value their ideas and feedback. Rather than deciding on your own what you should be focusing on, suddenly you have many brains to think about it. You want to make sure as much as possible that you will invest your time and energy in activities which will deliver high return. Don't take their feedback as negative criticism, but appreciate it as positive feedback to make sure your time and energy is funnelled in the right direction.

2. You want to communicate your priorities to the rest of the team and understand each others' priorities, so that everyone understands what each person will be focusing on. When a group of people are clear on a common goal and on how each of them can contribute to it, they become a real team.

3. You want to synergise on some projects. When you present your high-impact activities, one of your colleagues might be able to help you or advise you if he or she has done something similar in the past.

It is important to be aware of what every one else is focusing on. I have seen several dysfunctional teams and very often each person has little understanding of what their colleagues are really doing.

If today was the last day of my life

This process, which will help you to align your day-to-day activities with your goals, is as relevant for your personal life as it is for your business life. On the personal side, once you are clear on your long-term goals, and what you want to achieve personally, you need to decide what you will focus on in the next few months to get closer to your dreams.

Remember the Chinese proverb 'The journey of a 1,000 miles start with the first step.' What are the steps you will take towards your goals in the next three months?

This looks like a simple process. In reality it is an important mind shift. Remember the quote from the speech Apple CEO Steve Jobs delivered at Stanford University in 2005:

> *'For the past 33 years, I have looked in the mirror every morning and asked myself: "If today was the last day of my life, would I want to do what I am about to do today?"*

> *'And whenever the answer has been "No" for too many days in a row, I know I need to change something ... almost everything.*

> *'All external expectations, all pride, all fear of embarrassment or failure — these things just fall away in the face of death, leaving only what is truly important.'*

This is what I call a mind shift — to ask yourself every day: 'Is this day what I really want it to be? Am I focused on what is very important for me?'

Again, the crossover between work and personal life is obvious there. Are you focusing at work and in your personal life on the things which will help you achieve your long-term goals?

We should ask ourselves these kinds of questions every day before deciding to stay another hour at work doing emails rather than going home to be with our kids and wife, before accepting a meeting which is a 'nice to' but not a 'must do' rather than spending this one-and-a-half hours on an important project for the company, before lazing on the couch in front of the TV at night rather than spending quality time with our partner or close friends or going to bed early to be in top form the next day.

So if we can't be bothered to ask ourselves once a quarter what we need to focus on, what is key for us, and to be clear on it on a daily basis, then we allow day-to-day crises, other people's priorities and trivial activities to drive our life. We are being a reactive follower rather than a proactive leader.

5.4 THE PROJECT PLAN

Plan to save time

Some of your high-impact activities might be specific projects. They will have a start date, a due date and specific objectives. It might be useful to do some planning on these projects before jumping straight away in the 'doing'.

Quite often I see people struggling to be clear on the key projects they want to focus on over the next quarter, and how to gain traction on them. They have decided to organise a key event, or work on a key project, but are not sure how to start.

The first step is often the hardest one. If you can put something into action, then little by little the momentum makes it easier to achieve your aim. And the first step I recommend is to plan.

Funny how the word planning is often regarded as investing time. I'm often told: 'I don't have the time to plan.' The opposite screams to me: you don't have the time not to plan. Planning is such a time saver; why on earth would you want not to invest a bit of time at the start of a project to save massive amount of time all the way through?

I like the famous saying: 'In order to go fast first you need to go slow.' This has never been truer than for planning.

I remember a discussion with a director of a major financial institution in Australia. We had worked with him and his team on effectiveness. A few weeks later I was catching up with him. He mentioned two projects he had been working on recently. For the first project he took the time to do the plan as we had worked on. When it was time to present to the key stakeholders, the project was well thought out and organised, the project was a success and so far well on track.

He also mentioned another project. Because of the speed of things, and being caught up with many day-to-day crises, he did not have the time to do much planning. He and his team rushed into the doing rather than stopping beforehand to do the planning. His feedback was clear:

'We got seriously bitten on this one. We had a meeting with key stakeholders and it went so wrong we had to completely redo the work and meet with the key stakeholders one by one afterwards to put the project back on track. We wanted to save one hour of planning time up front, but we lost countless hours because of it afterwards.'

The point is simple. Save time, plan beforehand.

And planning is not limited to big projects and highly paid project managers using powerful software. Recruiting someone is a project, as is inducting the person, organising an event with a few clients, launching a product, and so on. Even going on vacation with your partner and kids is a project. I'd rather do a bit of planning prior to leaving rather than arrive at destination for my holiday and waste my precious two weeks because of poor planning.

Plan to reach the expected outcome

But the reason to plan is not only to save time. Possibly more importantly, planning increases dramatically your chance to achieve your desired goals.

There is an interesting theory called 'the butterfly effect', a term coined to describe the findings of MIT meteorologist Edward Lorenz while researching chaos theory. The story tells that a tiny event such as a butterfly moving its wing in San Francisco can create a storm in Shanghai. The idea is that a small event at the start of a project can have dramatic impact on the end results.

I don't know about the butterfly, but Edwards Deming, an American statistician widely credited on improving US production during World War II and in Japan afterwards, was very clear on the importance of planning.

He demonstrated that the start of a project — the planning phase at the beginning — was absolutely crucial to the desired outcomes. Deming showed that 85% of the success of a project is linked to how well the start of the project is thought out and planned.

There is a common saying: 'By failing to plan you are planning to fail.' I think it is very relevant in our busy business world. We are so busy running after daily issues and crises that we don't take enough time to plan and we end up with new crisis. It's a vicious circle.

The simple steps of planning

In my career, I have been involved in large and small projects. I have worked on big launches where we had to plan every detail with care, and like everyone I am involved daily with fairly simple and straightforward projects.

Whatever the size of a project, I have found there are three simple steps to plan a project:

1. The scope — what are you trying to achieve?
2. The breakdown — brainstorm all the steps to get there
3. The plan — organise these ideas in a simple plan and in your diaries

STEP 1: THE SCOPE

In his book *The 7 Habits of Highly Effective People®*, Stephen Covey defines the first step to effectiveness as 'start with the end in mind.' When planning a project, be clear on what you want to do and what outcomes you want to achieve.

More important than the how, which will come in steps two and three, the why is crucial to anything we do. To be effective and successful, you should always question why you are doing things, why you are investing time and resources on a project. Are the outcomes worth it, or are you better off doing something else?

Too often we see companies and teams investing time into projects which are not key to the overall success of the company, or which impede them from doing something much more important.

I suggest before any projects to answer the following questions:

- What are the objectives of this project?
- What are the expected outcomes?
- Your motivation/purpose — what's in it for you?
- What will be the long-term impact of this project?

Objectives and outcomes

Be as specific as you can. A simple way to answering this first question is to use the following format: By (specific date) to do (specific set of actions) in order to achieve (measurable outcomes).

Be very clear and very specific on the outcomes. Do not write, 'I want to grow our revenue', but 'By the end of the year to have segmented our client base into A, B and C clients and focus 70% of our sales resources on A clients in order to increase our revenue by 30% compare to last year.' Do not write 'I want to improve the call centre process,' but 'By April, I want to design a new call centre process in order to reduce missed calls from 25% to 5% and waiting time from one and a half hours to twenty seconds.'

No one gets very motivated by the set of actions to be undertaken. Being clear on the outcomes, on why we are launching ourselves in a set of actions, is much more motivating.

I remember working with a call centre. The manager had originally written, 'I want to implement a new call procedure for the call centre.' When she explained the project to the team in the room, I could feel people thinking, 'Another project; another change of process, so what …?'

I pushed the manager to be clearer on the why, on the outcomes expected. After a bit of thinking, she came down with, 'By the end of October to have worked with the call centre team to implement a new call procedure in order to save each person in the call centre one hour per day.'

You should have seen the face of all the call centre people. Now she was talking! Now they were keen to be involved in the project. Just by rephrasing her objective and being clear on the ultimate goal and outcome of the project, she suddenly had all the team on board.

■ Motivation and purpose

Your motivation will be your fuel during the project. Understanding why this project is important for you — what's in it for you — is key. The German philosopher Nietzsche wrote, 'If you have a strong why, you will find a how.' Before discussing how to do it, be clear on *why* you need to do it.

What is your personal motivation to achieve this project? Is it financial, career, personal satisfaction …? How will you feel at the end of the project if you have achieved it?

■ Long-term impact

Another question to ask yourself is about the long-term impact of the project on your performance and the performance of your business. If you are involved in many projects, being clear on the long-term impact of each will help you to prioritise all your projects.

■ Write the scope

Before rushing myself into any project, I take a piece of paper and answer these simple questions. It only takes me a couple of minutes, but always brings clarity to why I need to do it. It also helps me to prioritise between all the projects I want to launch.

What is clear in your mind you can easily write down on paper. If you are struggling to write it down, it is probably not that clear in your mind.

Whether you are working alone on a project or not, I suggest to always write on paper the scope of your project. If you can explain it simply and clearly to someone else who is not a specialist in your area, and if this person understands clearly what you want to do and why, you have probably a good scope. If not, you probably need to go back to the drawing board and redo it.

■ Share the scope

If you are working with a team, it is even more crucial to have a clear scope. Everyone needs to be clear on what you are all trying to achieve. You don't want to have a team spending time and energy on a project only to discover in the end that there was a misunderstanding at the start and you have in fact worked in different directions. And, believe me, this happens more often than not.

The scope is also a great tool to use during a project to refocus people including yourself and to include newcomers to the project. On projects which last a few months, I have been surprised how useful it is for everyone to revisit the scope to make sure we are still heading in the right direction.

If there are a few people working together on a project, outline the scope together at the beginning. And if you need to involve new people during the life of a project, show them the scope. Make sure they are clear on why you are all doing this.

■ Practise

By now you should know that I do not believe in learning by listening or reading. I am a firm believer in the value of practising. So let's apply these concepts.

Select a project which is current and important. You may want to do this on your own or involve a few people relevant to the project. Use the following template and answer the questions in it, keeping in mind what we have discussed.

PROJECT NAME

_____

start date: end date:

_____

PROJECT SCOPE

Objective [By (date) to do (activities) in order to achieve (specific outcomes)]

_____
_____
_____
_____
_____

Results/outcomes expected [be clear on why you are doing this project]

_____
_____
_____
_____
_____

Purpose/motivation [what's in it for me?]

_____
_____
_____
_____
_____

Long-term impact on the performance

_____
_____
_____
_____
_____

People involved and resources needed

_____
_____
_____
_____
_____

Figure 5.9: Project scope

STEP 2: THE BREAKDOWN

Once you are clear on what you are trying to get — your objective for the project — it's time to be creative and consider how you are going to get there. In the scope you want the logical side of your brain, sometimes called the left side, to do the work. Now, let your creative side express itself.

The aim now is to write down all the tasks/steps/actions to be completed to reach your objective. You want to breakdown this project into simple and single tasks.

There are several ways of doing this, from taking a piece of paper and writing all the tasks you think of one after the other, to writing your ideas as a drawing on a single piece of paper.

The method I prefer and recommend is the brain dumping one. Take a large piece of paper, ideally an A3 sheet, and write at the centre the name of the project. For example, you are in charge of recruiting a new account manager.

Figure 5.10: Beginning a 'brain dump' — planning objectives

Then try to think of all the steps to organise this recruitment. For example you will need to be clear on the role and write the position description, advertise for the role both internally and externally, organise the recruitment process with interviews, start thinking about the induction of this new employee, and so on. Write all these steps on the paper:

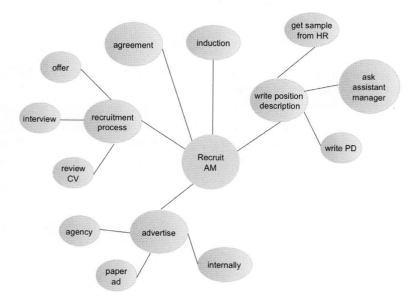

Figure 5.11: 'Brain dump' — use mind mapping to list tasks

In doing your brain dump you need to think as a project manager not as an expert. What I mean by this is: you are not trying to find solutions yet, you are just thinking of all the tasks which need to be done to get to your end goals.

Let's illustrate the difference between thinking like an expert and thinking like a project manager, using the steps called 'write a position description'. If you think like an expert, you will start brainstorming on the right position description:

- Very strong knowledge of the finance industry
- In charge of growing our large clients x, y and z
- In charge of prospecting new clients in a specific area
- Very strong negotiating skills
- A real team player
... and so on.

You are starting to answer the question.

If you think like a project manager, you will brainstorm on the tasks to be done to get the position description:

- Ask HR for copies of existing position description in sales
- Ask the feedback from the existing sales team
- Then write the position description

Practise

If you started a scope on a specific project, take a piece of paper, the larger the better, ideally A3, and do the brain dump on this specific project. Take the time to write all your ideas.

Use a pencil as you will probably have to modify things until you are happy with your brain dump. You may have to do a first draft and then, if difficult to read, redo it properly on a second draft.

STEP 3: THE PROJECT PLAN – BRINGING ORDER

Once you have completed this breakdown of steps and tasks, you are now ready for the last phase: the project plan. You are going to put some order into all these tasks. Take a few different coloured pens and follow these steps:

1. Take a first coloured pen and order each task, from the first that needs to be done to the last. Decide which tasks needs to be done first, which tasks will follow, and so on. I suggest using multiples of five to avoid mistakes. Start by putting a '5' next to the first task you need to do, then a '10' next to the following one and so on by multiple of five.

The reason why I suggest using multiples of five is to avoid having to start all over again if you realise you have forgotten to number a task. If the task you have forgotten should be done after task numbered '35' and before task numbered '40', simple put '37' in front of this new task.

2. Take another coloured pen and write next to each task how long this task will take to be completed and who will be in charge of doing it. For example you might say that task '55' will need one hour to be completed and should be done by Mary.

3. Take another coloured pen and put a date next to each task according to when this task should be done. It is easy to give dates for tasks to be completed soon; harder for tasks to be completed in a few months. The further away it is, the more approximate the date will be.

In doing step three, you can either start with the first task, and move forward until you have reached the last task, or start with the last task if you have a compulsory due date and revert backward until you have reached the first task.

Starting from the last task and going backward could prove challenging. You could end up with a date for the first task which is in the past. This means you should have started the project earlier to do all you want to do. You have now to decide to push the due date or, if you can't, what you will accelerate and which tasks you will eliminate.

4. Once the three previous steps are completed, you need to move all this into a project plan and in your calendar. If you are working on a fairly small project, you may not need a project plan, and copying all the dates in your calendar and the calendar of others involved in the project will be enough.

If you are working on a mid-size project, you may want to create a project plan on a Word document or Excel® spreadsheet:

Project Plan

Task	time	when	who	tick

Figure 5.12: Project plan

If you are working on a very large project, you may want to use project management software such as Microsoft Project.

But in all cases, whether you are working on a small, medium or large project, ask everyone to then move all the tasks in which they are involved to their calendar. This is a very important step. As a result, all the tasks and actions you have to do over the next few months will be in your calendar as well as in the calendar of all the people involved.

It always surprises me to see that most people have quite a few things booked in their calendar for the one or two weeks ahead, and not much after. It looks as though, according to their calendar, they have much available time in the weeks to come. The reality is often different. They might be committed to several key projects and have very little time available. But because they have not included in their calendar the tasks and actions they have to do, they do not realise how committed they are. And they book other things, such as meetings, leaving little space for these important actions.

Planning — the payback

Doing a proper scope, breakdown and project plan can take a little bit of time. But the payback is huge. Once you have realised how beneficial it is to plan, you will be very reluctant to do without it.

Project planning is first an important step to being more effective at a personal level. You are deciding right back at the beginning, in the scope, which projects will have a high impact on your performance and therefore which projects you should focus on. Then you are mapping out all the actions to achieve the desired outcomes, and making these actions a 'must' in your calendar.

Project planning is also an important step to be effective as a team. Doing the scope, breakdown and project plan as a team brings clarity to all on what needs to be done and why, who is accountable for what and when. Everyone understands where they fit into the overall project, and how important their part is to the success of this project. Everyone understands that delaying their part will have a cascading effect on the whole time frame.

In many years of coaching individuals and teams, I have found that people do not suffer from lack of time; they suffer from lack of focus and planning. If you are struggling for time, take the time to plan.

6

" Particularly the effective week has helped me feel much more in control of my life and enabled me to easily juggle family priorities and business. I now never feel guilty when I am at home enjoying family time as it is diarized time!

Sales Program Manager
SingTel Optus

Chapter 6

PLAN WEEKLY: MAKE THEM A 'MUST'

6.1 PUT YOUR BIG ROCK FIRST

One of the most powerful stories in the area of time management is the big rock story. It has been told often and in different ways by many specialists in the area of effectiveness, performance and time management such as Steven Covey in his book titled *First Think First*.

The story says that one day a university professor was teaching a course on time management. At the start of class, he placed a large jar and a bag full of big rocks on his table, then started to fill the jar with the big rocks. When the jar was full, he asked the students, 'Is the jar full?' They answered yes.

From under his desk the professor pulled out a bag full of pebbles and started pouring the pebbles in the jar in between the big rocks. Once again when the jar was full of pebbles, he asked the students, 'Is the jar full?' This time the students understood the trick and answered no.

'You are right,' said the professor as he pulled a bag of sand from under his desk. He poured the sand into the jar in between the big rocks and the pebbles. When the jar was full of sand, he asked the students, 'Is the jar full?' They answered no.

'You are right again,' was his answer as he pulled a bottle of water from under the table. As previously, he filled the jar with water. Once the jar was full of water, he asked once more, 'Is the jar full?' This time the students are a bit hesitant but agree the jar looks pretty full.

'You are right. The jar is now full,' said the professor. Then he asked, 'What is the moral of this story?' As the course was on time management, one of the students explained that the moral is that we always believe we are very busy but can always fit smaller tasks in between what we do, much more that we initially thought.

'Not at all,' said the professor. 'The moral of this story is to always put your big rock first. If I had taken the same jar, put first exactly the same amount of water I have just put in, then exactly the same amount of sand I have just put in, then exactly the same amount of pebbles I have just put in, I would not have been able to fit half of the big rocks I have put in.'

Your big rocks are the things that are important for you. In your job big rocks are your activities and projects which will have a high impact long term on your performance and on the performance of your business. In your personal life your big rocks are your personal life goals as well as the people who are important to you — your partner, your children, your health, your dreams and so on.

The moral of this story is that if you do not put your big rock first, the pebbles, sand and water of life will take over. If you do not make your important business and personal projects a 'must', the little things of life — the pebbles, sand and water — will take over.

How often have I heard someone complaining about working long hours, but feeling completely empty and frustrated at the end of the day as they are wondering what exactly they have achieved? They are working hard but they know intuitively that they spend most of their days on 'pebbles, sand and water' and do not focus on any big rocks.

How sad it is to hear someone saying they worked too hard and did not spend enough time with their partner or kids. Now they are divorced and their kids have grown up. They had real big rocks called 'my partner' or 'my kids', but they did not put them first.

I am often asked to do speeches on the topic of efficiency and effectiveness. One question I sometime ask at the start of the speech is, 'What would you do if you had one extra hour per day?' Usually the answers are: 'More time with my family, more time to look after my health, more time to travel,' and so on. So many people do not put their big rocks first, only to realise this important lesson when it's too late.

Hyrum Smith, the CEO of Franklin Quest Co, an American time management company, tells a moving story which illustrates the importance of putting your big rocks first. An executive from Merrill Lynch in the US attended a seminar run by Hyrum, during which they spoke about what really matters for each of us, about each person's really big rocks. A year later Hyrum received one of the most emotional letters he had ever received. In this letter, the executive explained how he had realised that although his son was truly important to him, he had not dedicated a lot of time to him. He was not doing anything with his son.

From the day of seminar, the executive decided he would focus much more on his son. They spent a lot of quality time together, and it was a truly rewarding experience for both of them. Then, the executive explained his son had died in a car crash a week ago. Although devastated, he was not experiencing any guilt and even felt some inner peace. Although he was grieving the loss of his son, he was not grieving the time he could have spent with him. He had dedicated a lot of time and love to his son recently.

You do not know how long your loved ones are going to be around. And you do not know how long you will be around. So do not wait until it's too late to focus on your big rocks. Spend time with the people who matter now; take action on your dreams now, not tomorrow.

The same concept applies in our business life. Whatever will have a high impact long term on your performance is a big rock. Do not procrastinate on it; start now and put the rest — the sand, pebbles and water — after.

Be selfish to be generous

'Be selfish to be generous' might appear as nonsense, a contradiction. I believe, on the contrary, that to be generous, to be there for others, you have to be personally well centred, well balanced.

It starts with you. It is hard to be generous and available for others if you are not clear on your core values and what's important for you.

History is full of amazing and generous people who have dedicated their lives to others: Mother Theresa, Ghandi or L'abbé Pierre. From what I have read and heard about each of them, they were people of strong values who knew what was important for them and what was not, who were able to make tough decisions.

When I write 'be selfish' I don't mean it in the sense of only thinking about yourself, but starting with you. Be clear on your values, be clear on your dream and goals, be clear on the people who really count and then you can really be generous.

For example, you need to be clear on the people who are important for you. Then you should be generous to them. I don't think a dad who does too much for others and who has no time for his loved wife and kids is generous. And he is certainly not successful, in my mind.

Your time is precious and limited. Be clear about what is key for you and then be generous. Not the other way around.

A few simple time management principles

Managing your time does not mean anything in itself. Focusing your time and energy on your big rocks, on what is important for you, on what will make you successful at a personal and business level … there is the key.

It is absolutely necessary to manage your time well. I should be able to ask you how you spent your time three weeks ago on Friday by bunches of 15 minutes — I raised this earlier — and you should be able to answer. If you can't, you are probably not as effective as you could be. Are you beginning to see how this kind of management can allow you to be proactive?

If you do not manage your time, you cannot be effective. You would be like an Olympic swimmer who wants to improve but does not measure his time during training. What gets measured gets managed. To improve you need first to understand what you are doing.

However, time management is not sufficient in itself. If you record your time very well, know how you spend it, but do not spend it on big rocks, on high-impact activities, you will not be effective and will not perform.

Effective people know their big rocks and manage their time to put their big rock first.

■ Think, plan, act

The process of managing your time effectively is fairly simple. You need to think yearly and quarterly about your big rocks. For your role, you need to define and review your high-impact activities every quarter. As mentioned previously, you need to write them every quarter.

Then you should plan weekly. We will review the process and some tools a little bit further, but the principle is to review your quarterly plan at least once a week, and to plan your time for the following week accordingly, putting your big rocks first.

Then it will be easy to be effective on a daily basis, to act in line with your quarterly plan. Your big rocks are planned in your diary; you are clear on what to do and need to act on it, to focus on it.

Plan and respect your big rock meetings

I cannot say this enough. 'Put your big rock first.' This is probably the best way to explain how to be effective. You need to be clear on your big rocks and make them a 'must'. They need to be written black and white in your diary. Your diary should be full of 'big rock meetings', many of them with yourself.

You should treat these big rock meetings as very, very important, as if you were having a meeting with a key client or one of the executives of your company. You should allocate enough time for these meetings, and not treat them as a quick one when you have time.

Why do we have so little respect for the meetings we plan with ourselves? Too often I have seen someone blocking a big rock meeting in their diary, only to find out they did something else instead.

Let me guess. If you have a meeting with a key client, would you decide to finish some small tasks instead? Would you arrive ten minutes late? Would you bring your laptop and take care of a few emails during the meeting? Would you make a few phone calls while your client is speaking to you? Of course not. So why do we do this when we have booked a meeting with ourselves in our diary? If you have a big rock meeting with yourself scheduled from 10:00 am until 12:00 pm, be there at 10:00 am. Better still, be there at 9:55 am. Start on time. Block interruptions. Stay focused.

Be effective with your big rock meetings. This might mean being realistic when is best to plan them. I suggest taking into consideration your biorhythm and the reality of your office. If your brain works better in the early morning, try to schedule your big rock thinking and creativity sessions during that time. If you know you are likely to be interrupted every three minutes at your desk, schedule your big rock meetings in a separate room or out of the office.

Be realistic (let me breathe!)

Once your big rocks are in your diary, you will realise how little time you have for the rest. Great. This will enable you to decide what you can and can't do.

'No' is a very important word in effectiveness. I quoted earlier the famous management consultant Peter Drucker: 'The key of strategy is omission.' Once your big rocks are in your diary, you will have a better understanding of how committed you are already if you want to perform, and you will be able to say no to many 'pebbles, sand and water' requests.

However you need to also be realistic on how much available time you have and how to organise it. I do not want you to jump from the 'empty calendar' to the 'crazy calendar'.

I suggest letting your calendar 'breathe'. Leave some time open in between every meeting. Allow your calendar to breathe, otherwise it will suffocate.

In part one, chapter three, I discussed the concept of 'let me breathe'. It is quite an important concept and therefore worth revisiting.

I often see people with what I call 'an empty calendar'. Apart from a few meetings with other people, they do not have anything else. It does not mean they are not busy, it just means they do not use their calendar as an effectiveness tool. Their diary looks empty but the reality is often different. They are very committed but it does not show in their diary.

On the other side of the scale I sometimes see people with a crazy calendar. Their diary is full of back-to-back meetings, most of them with other people and a few with themselves. They rush from one meeting to another one. If one meeting goes overtime, they will be late to the next one. They have very little time available for unexpected problems, very little time for their staff or peers, and no time for all the little things we have to do every day.

	the empty calendar	let me breathe	the crazy calendar
8 am		team meeting	team meeting
9 00			
10 00	meeting with client	prepare document for executive committee	1.1 with John
			marketing steering committee
11 00		marketing steering committee	
12 pm			lunch with client
		lunch	
1 00			
2 00	internal meeting	1.1 with John	performance review with Steve
			meeting with Mike to prepare offsite
3 00			
		prepare proposal for client	prepare proposal for client
4 00			
			prepare document for executive committee
5 00			

Figure 6.1: The 'let me breathe' calendar

A calendar that is allowed to 'breathe' offers a happy medium. Your calendar should be full of big rock meetings, some with people and many with yourself. In between each meeting you should allocate a bit of time, a breather.

However well organised we are, we all need time for interruptions, crises and to do all the little things such as returning phone calls, checking messages and so on. How much time you need per day will depend on your role and your personality. Consider your role. If you're an executive who is supposed to be more proactive than reactive, you might only need thirty minutes' breathing time in between meetings. If you're a PA you might need two hours of breathing time between each meeting.

Your breathing time will allow you to do a few things:

■ Have a bit of time available if a meeting runs five minutes overtime
■ Debrief each meeting and organise the actions decided during this meeting
■ Do some of the little quick tasks we all have to do on a daily basis, such as returning phone calls
■ Be available for quick questions and interruptions
■ Prepare for the next meeting if necessary

Allow for these breathing times during the day. Otherwise you will finish the day stressed and frustrated because you did not make room for all the small things that occur every day.

Most people underestimate the time that ought to be allowed each day for unplanned activities, for reacting. In my experience even the most organised people need at least two hours per day of unplanned/reactive time.

If you are working ten hours per day, you need to leave at least two hours unplanned, often more. This means you can only plan eight hours per day, not ten.

■ Let me breathe to re-energise

It is also important to recognise that we can't work ten hours solid flat out. Well you can, but your level of energy and concentration will decrease. You will take more time to do your job as you get tired and you will increase your likelihood to make mistakes.

In his book *The Power of Full Engagement*, John Loehr explains how he started studying sport people and performance. They wanted to understand what set apart the great tennis players from the rest. To start with, they decided to observe some of the top players of the time: Pete Sampras, Jim Courrier and Bruguera. They spent hours observing how they were playing and could not find any specific difference to explain the difference of performance.

Then came the breakthrough. They decided to observe these players when they were not playing, between points and sets. To their surprise they found a significant difference to the rest.

While not aware of it, these top players had built almost exactly the same set of routines between points. They were using time between points to recover. Their heart rate was dropping by as much as 20 beats per minute while other players remained at the same heart rate. Although this was a small difference between points, after a two- to three-hour game it started making a big difference.

This enabled them to draw some interesting parallels with work in an office. In the early 1950s, researchers discovered that during the night and the day we are going through 90- to 120-minute cycles. This is quite well known when it comes to our sleeping cycles; less when it comes to our daily rhythms. During the day, every 90 to 120 minutes, the body needs a period of rest and recovery. We may experience the desire to yawn, to stretch and difficulty in concentrating. We can fight against it by flooding our body with stress hormones. This is fine once in a while, but if that's our normal modus operandi, we are slowly building up toxins in our body.

In short, you will struggle to be fully concentrated and on top of your performance if you work ten hours straight. You need to take breaks during the day and re-energise yourself. Go for a walk. Get some fresh air and sun. Change your ideas and forget work for a little while.

This is not time 'wasted'. On the contrary, you will achieve more during your work hours. Think about how quickly you can resolve an issue or do a difficult piece of work early in the morning compared to doing the same situation late afternoon or straight after lunch.

As mentioned earlier, Fast Company magazine asked successful professionals how to avoid being burnt out. Nearly all of them explained how they have put in place daily and weekly routines to regularly renew themselves.

■ Be creative rather than bound to convention

You need to be creative with how you manage time and avoid being bound by either conventions or what others think. Do not feel you have to follow the same rhythm and routine as everyone else if it's not the best for you.

For example, it might work better for you to start very early in the morning and leave early. Or you might find it very beneficial twice a week to go to the gym at lunch time, or once a day to walk for between 30 minutes to one hour to get some fresh air.

You might decide to work often from home or not at your desk to reduce interruptions and be more focused on high-impact activities, on big rocks. Some people that we coach decide after the journey to work far more often at home, and the impact on their productivity is huge.

However it is often easier said than done. Many employers will say they are open to flexibility with their white collar workers, but in reality would regard someone working from home as at least slightly suspicious. And most of us would feel uncomfortable or guilty in leaving our desk to go for a walk, to take one-and-a-half hours to go to the gym or to decide to spend a whole day working at home.

I know the feeling. When not coaching, I leave the office around 4:30 pm to go home. Over the years I have found that one of the best times to do my calls is between 5:30 pm and 6:30 pm. Many people that I call are managers and executives. After 5:30 pm their PA is often gone and thus less likely to be at their desk. So this time slot works well for me. The problem is that if I leave my office at 6:30 pm, I will be home late, my youngest daughter will be in bed and I will have missed dinner with the family.

So I decided a new rhythm which works great for me. When I'm not coaching in the late afternoon, I leave the office around 4:30 pm, I beat the traffic and I am home around 5:15 pm. Then I do my calls from home. At 6:15 pm, when I hang up from my last call, I am ready to be with my family. I am already home.

Although I do not report to anyone — I manage my own business — at the beginning I was feeling almost guilty in front of the rest of the team to leave that early. Although this is a rhythm which works very well for me, I was reluctant to do it because of what others might think.

You need to think about a time management routine that is best for you, which will enhance your performance, even if it is not 100% conventional. Don't be afraid to do things differently.

I would even go further. In some cases you should challenge the status quo in order to be creative; you should think differently and act differently in order to put yourself in the best performance rhythm. In his book *How to think like Leonardo da Vinci*, author Michael Gelb ask an interesting question to executives: 'Where are you when you get your best ideas?'

Most common answers are: 'In the shower, in my bed, on holiday, walking in nature, listening to music.' Gelb writes that 'Almost no-one mentions "at work".' He then explains 'the greatest geniuses sometime accomplish more when they work less.'

How much value do you bring when you are only reacting — dealing with your emails, answering interruptions and jumping from one crisis to another one? Most of us would bring so much more value to our role and business if we would spend more time thinking, more time relaxing, more time being creative.

Think about yourself at your best, when you are full of energy to think and create, and organise your time accordingly, even if it's not exactly how others would expect you to.

6.2 PROTECT YOUR BIG ROCKS — IMPLEMENT YOUR EFFECTIVE WEEK

I would like to introduce now a simple methodology to increase your effectiveness, your focus on your big rocks. I call this process the effective week. Remember, the one key factor of success — of effectiveness — is to make your big rock a must.

The aim of this process is to assess whether you are being realistic about your big rocks, about the amount of time you should spend on them to perform, and then to organise your time accordingly.

Below is a simple form I suggest using for this exercise. Make a copy of this form or reproduce it on a piece of paper.

Meetings with self		Meetings with others	
name	hours/week	name	hours/week
total	0	total	0
interruptions, crises			0
unplanned			
others			0
total needed	0		
total available			

Figure 6.2: Implement your effective week

Think about a week where you are very effective and on top of your priorities. I am not talking about a specific week like next week or the week before. Think about a week where you are not running frantically but in control and proactive.

Step 1: meetings with others

List the regular meetings with others, either already planned or which should be planned. You might be part of a regular weekly meeting with your team but you might also decide you should have a regular weekly or fortnightly catch-up with a few people. You might also decide you should be at least one day per week on the field, meeting with clients, or have two meetings per day with clients.

At the end of this process you will have to make some tough decisions on which meetings you should be part of and which meetings you cannot join. For the moment, list all your meetings with others.

This could include:

- regular meetings you attend
- regular one-on-one with your team or your boss
- regular meetings with clients and prospects
- meetings with other colleagues to work on key projects
... and so on.

For each, estimate the amount of time you need to spend to be effective. Don't write, 'I need nine hours per week with clients,' but, 'I need to have six client meetings per week of one-and-a-half hours each.'

Beware of not forgetting some of your obvious but not necessarily weekly responsibilities. I was coaching a manager from a bank and we did a first draft of his effective week. In our next session two weeks after, he was struggling with his time. His effective week looked all well and good on paper, but the reality was different. He was struggling to spend any time on his big rocks.

We discussed the issue and he mentioned he was involved in a few conventions from time to time. They were happening quite regularly but not on a weekly or fortnightly basis. I asked him to estimate the amount of time he was spending on the field with advisers and sales people, both in presenting to them during conventions and coaching them. After assessing the number of days needed per year, we found out this was taking more than a third of his time. Then I asked how much time he needed to prepare all this. Here we were back in calculation mode, to find out in the end he was spending nearly 50% of his time doing this. He had forgotten to cater for an activity which was requiring 50% of his time.

Be honest. Be thorough. Do not forget key aspects of your role.

Once this is done, calculate the number of hours per week needed.

Step 2: meetings with self

Try to assess how much time per week you would need ideally to spend on your own on specific big rock projects. This could include key projects, personal or staff development, creativity and innovation — any key activities that are not with other people.

This is harder to estimate than meetings with others. However, I have found by experience that most people know how much time they should dedicate per day to their specific projects.

Again, try to be specific. Don't write, 'I need about twenty hours per week,' but, 'I need two sessions of two hours per day on my specific projects to be effective.'

Keep in mind that this is an estimate. You are designing your effective week, your ideal week.

If you are wearing different distinctive hats in your role, you can try to estimate the time you need to spend per hat each week. For example this would give:

- Innovation and creativity   4 x 2 hours per week
- Sales strategy and account planning   3 x 2 hours per week
- Strategy, long-term planning   2 x 2 hours per week
- Calls: 1 hour per day   5 x 1 hour per week

Again, once this is done, calculate the amount of hours per week needed.

This could include:

- time spent on key projects
- regular phone calls you have to make
- time to prepare your meetings and do your administrative work
- email time on a daily basis
... and so on.

Once this is done, calculate the number of hours per week needed.

Step 3: 'me time'

Being effective also means knowing what is important for you, what 'me time' you need to factor in during or around your work hours. The most obvious one is the time you should allocate every day for lunch, but 'me time' could be much more than lunch time.

For example if you have decided you should go to the gym twice a week at lunch time, write 'gym 2 x 1.5 hours'. If you want to pick up your kids from school once a week, write down when and at what time you need to leave.

To be effective you need to put your big rocks first. This is true not only for your business big rocks but also your personal ones. Your health is a big rock, your family, wife or husband, kids are big rocks. Your real friends are big rocks. They should be a must. Don't forget your personal big rocks. Life is senseless without them.

Step 4: unplanned/reactive time

One of the biggest challenges for most people is to realise how much time they spend reacting, in unplanned activities. We all need to have some unplanned time every day, time to respond to unexpected crises, time to deal with interruptions, time to do all the thousand little things we need to do on a daily basis.

When trying to organise their time, most people do not take this into account. If they decide to work ten hours one day, they will plan ten hours of activities, and often more.

Even when I ask them to estimate the amount of time needed per day for unplanned activities, most people completely underestimate what they really need.

In my experience people who are very focused and do not suffer from day-to-day interruptions still need at least one-and-a-half to two hours of unplanned time per day. And most people need more than this.

Be honest about the amount of time you need per day for unplanned activities.

Step 5: others

Let's be honest: on top of all the above there will always be other things which will happen. It could be an internal meeting you have been requested to attend, a farewell party for a departing colleague, a training session you need to join, or similar.

Try to estimate how much time you need to cater for events during your week which are not part of your routine.

Step 6: calculate and decide

Now is time to do the math. Calculate the amount to time needed by adding the total of step 1 + step 2 + step 3 + step 4 + step 5. Calculate how many hours per week you need to be effective, to realistically do well all what you need to do.

Then calculate how much time you have available, how much time you want to work per week. I suggest asking yourself how many hours you realistically want to work, not how many hours you should work.

If the two totals match, well done. You are ready to implement your effective week in your diary. If they don't, join the club. You are not alone. Most people that I coach are with you. This is what I call the Houston symptom — when it is time to say 'Houston, we have a problem,' and find a solution.

Step 7: Houston, we have a problem

It's time to make some tough choices. I suggest first to be very clear on your big rocks. Ask yourself which activities are critical to your performance; which will have a long-term high impact on your performance and the performance of your business.

Take your compass plan and review the few activities you need to focus on in order to perform. Review the activities to which you should dedicate 80% of your time. You want to fill your calendar with these activities, to lock your time around your big rocks in order to avoid spending too much time on pebbles, sand and water.

Take a red pen and put a red dot next to each of theses. Ideally you do not want to reduce the time allocated to these high-impact activities.

Review all your activities. Decide what you need to do and what you can either avoid or delegate. What you can say no to? This is a difficult and confronting exercise, which in some cases might require some discussions with your manager.

But there is one thing you can be sure of, the math does not lie. If the amount of hours needed to be effective are higher that the number of hours available, you will struggle to be effective and to perform.

Most people end up spending their time between ongoing internal meetings, last minute meetings, and unplanned time responding to crises, interruptions and out-of-routine activities. Because specific big rocks projects can often be put on the back burner, they end up spending very little time on proactive activities and 'me time'. They are not effective.

Take the time needed. Review and discuss with the right people. Decide which big rocks you need to focus on and make sure your time needed to be effective equals your available time.

Meetings with self		Meetings with others	
name	hours/week	name	hours/week
Business		1.1 meeting with manager	1 x 0.5 hr
High impact projects time	5 x 2 hr	1.1 meeting with direct reports	4 x 0.5 hr
thinking time	3 x 1.5 hr	weekly team meeting	1 x 1.5 hr
per hat time	4 x 1.5 hr	High Impact projects meeting	3 x 1 hr
emails	5 x 1 hr	client meetings	5 x 1 hr
calls	5 x 0.5 hr	joint field time	0.5 day
etc …			
Me time			
lunch	5 x 0.5 hr		
gym/yoga	2 x 1 hr		
pick up kids	Thu 5 pm		
total	T1	total	T2
unplanned	2 hr per day		T3
reactive time			
others	3 planned meetings of 1 hr per week		T4
total needed	T1 + T2 + T3 + T4		
total available	45	office time – 8:30 am to 5:30 pm	

Figure 6.3: Getting real on priorities

Step 8: Book recurrent meetings in your calendar

Now is time to implement your 'effective week' in your calendar. Most people only have in their calendar as recurrent meetings some of their ongoing meetings with others such as the internal meetings they attend weekly or fortnightly.

I suggest implementing as many big rocks as possible as recurrent meetings. For example, if you would like to spend two meetings with yourself of two hours each day on your specific big rock projects, decide when is the best time to do so, go into your calendar in Outlook, Lotus or whatever system you are using and create recurrent meetings call 'big rock time' or 'key project time' at the time which suits you the best.

If you are in sales and need to make one hour of phone calls every day to clients and prospects, decide when and block your time to do it. Ask yourself what time of the day is ideal for your calls and book a recurrent meeting with yourself.

You should do the same for your 'me time'. If you have written that you would like to go twice per week to the gym, decide when and book recurrent meetings for this. If you have decided that every Wednesday morning you would like to take the kids to school, again block your time in your calendar as a recurrent meeting.

Do not worry if some of these recurrent meetings clash with existing meetings in the next few weeks. Next I will suggest reviewing your calendar on a weekly basis and changing what does not work.

In scheduling your big rocks in your calendar, think about your biorhythm; think about when is the best time for you to do them. I am a morning person and I have blocked every morning from 8:00 am until 10:00 am to work on my big rocks. I get into the office around 7:40 every morning, do a few things and get ready to focus on my big rocks by 8:00 am. I know this is the best time for me, that my brain works better at that time.

A lot of these recurrent appointments will be meetings with yourself. Why not block this time, protecting it to make sure you have enough time to work on your big rocks? Respecting the time you plan to work on these things will have a great impact on your performance and the performance of your business. You are making your big rocks a 'must'.

Below is an example of an effective week.

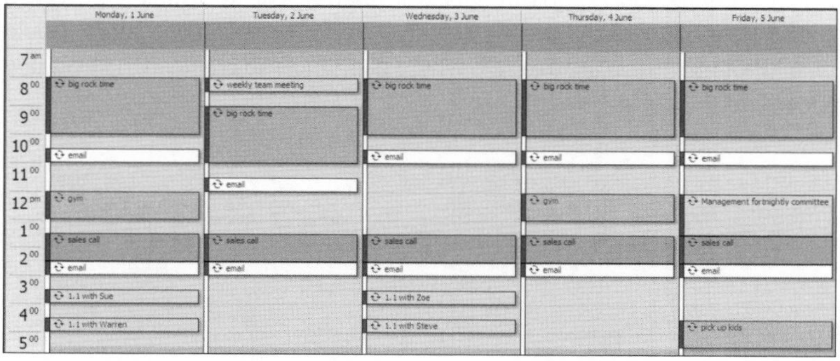

Figure 6.4: An effective weekly plan in Outlook

In this example the person has decided to block two hours every morning for his big rocks and one hour every afternoon for his phone calls. It is unlikely that every week will be exactly mirroring your effective week. But if you manage to keep 80% of your effective week this will be a great achievement. You need to protect your time for important activities, those which will have a long-term impact on your performance.

When I do this exercise with the people I coach, I often hear the same comments: 'Gee, I can see now that 60% to 70% of my time is already committed every week.' For most people, the next few days are often quite busy in their calendar but if you look a few weeks ahead, their calendar is nearly empty. The reality is very different. If they want to do their job properly, 60% to 70% of their time is already committed. To be effective, they must put their big rocks first; the rest will need to fit around those. Protect your time. Block your time in advance for important activities.

Make it visual and lively: colour code your calendar

Microsoft Outlook enables you to colour code your calendar. You can decide on a few categories and apply a different colour to each of them. For example you can choose to colour:

- your big rocks time/creativity time in green
- your internal meetings in grey
- your sales time in red
- your personal time in blue

Everyone will have different categories which will work best for them. Do not have too many of them otherwise it will become difficult to see. Creating four or five categories is probably right.

Colour coding your appointments will enable you to visualise how you spend most of your time every week. If sales is your main area, there should be a lot of red. If you are in a role where planning and creativity is key, there should be a lot of green.

6.3 BE IN CONTROL — PLAN WEEKLY RELIGIOUSLY

The last step of the process to make your big rock a must, and one of the most important ones, is the weekly review. Every week we all have many things to do, many things to achieve. And having all these to do in our head, or at best on a long 'to do' list on a piece of paper, does not guarantee you will achieve them all.

Pause once a week to plan the following week

You need to sit down once a week, review what you have to do, prioritise by impact/value if possible rather than by urgency, decide what you can physically do and, more importantly, what you can't do, and organise your calendar accordingly.

This is an absolute must to be effective and feel in control. Once you are used to this weekly routine, you will not be able to do without it. A week with no weekly planning is stressful, ineffective and often painful.

You need between thirty minutes and an hour every week to do this well. Each Friday morning, or Monday morning if this works better for you, review the following week. Most people that I coach sit down on Friday to review their following week. However for some people the following week is completely booked out and they should review and plan their time two weeks in advance, or more if needed.

Be proactive: think long-term impact and not deadlines

When it is time to do your weekly plan, first review your compass plan. Put yourself in a 'high-impact mode' and check what you need to achieve to perform this quarter rather than only focusing on what's urgent. Review your key projects, your compass plan, your big rocks. Your aim is to spend the majority of your time on these high-impact activities, on these big rocks.

Commit yourself: be clear on the what and when

It's a very important process to decide what you will do, what you must do, decide when and write it down in your diary. Even if you have protected your time with your effective week as suggested previously, you should not leave your recurrent meetings as 'high-impact time' or 'key project time' for the following week. You need to commit and write precisely what you will work on during that time.

Several researchers confirm that specifying what you will do and when dramatically increases the likelihood of success. Loehr and Schwartz offer two studies as examples. In one of these studies the researchers wanted to test the participation in a fitness program offered to non-exercising college students.

At first the students were given information on how exercising would reduce the vulnerability to heart diseases. As a result the participation to the fitness program increased from 29% to 39%. When this information was followed by a request to tell when and where they would exercise, participation increased to 91%.

In another study, a group of drug addicts were going through a withdrawal program. As part of helping them to find a job post their rehabilitation, they were asked to write a short résumé. One group was asked to write a resumé before a specific deadline. None of the participants did it. Another group was given the same task but also all participants were asked to specify when and where they would do it. Eighty per cent of the participants did it.

Planning your week is such an important step. You are making a commitment with yourself regarding how you will use this time by writing it clearly in your calendar. If you don't write precisely what you must do, you will be at risk of filling this time with water, sand and pebbles.

You just need to plan your week once a week. Then on a daily basis you do not have to plan or make decisions about 'what do I do now?' You simply need to act on what you previously decided.

I remember the feedback from one of my clients. He explained to me that because he had organised a few meetings with himself in his diary, he had felt committed to do it. He would have felt guilty not to do these meetings. He had made an agreement with himself about what to focus on to be successful, and he knew he had to stick with it even though there were plenty of opportunities to get distracted.

The weekly plan form

Here is a form I suggest using for this exercise. If you use a pencil, you can use the same form every week.

Weekly List – Specific Projects			
name	hours/week	name	hours/week
		total	0
Ongoing Responsibilities			
name	hours/week	name	hours/week
		total	0
interruptions, crises			0
unplanned			
others			
total needed	0		
total available			

Figure 6.5: The weekly plan form

Step 1: list all your 'to do'/specific projects

List all the key projects you need to work on the following week. Also list all the large and small tasks you need to do. For each, allocate the right amount of time you need to spend. Be precise — if you need to spend 3 x 1.5 hours on a project, don't write 4.5 hours but 3 x 1.5 hours.

You can either write all your tasks in one long list or segment them per 'hat', per responsibility.

When all is done, calculate your total for proactive time/specific projects and tasks.

Weekly List – Specific Projects			
name	hours/week	name	hours/week
hat 1 – Management		**hat 3 – Sales**	
induction Sue	2	proposal for AAA	1
review KPI	1	account planning	1.5
hat 2 – Strategy		review Compass Plan	
prepare offsite	2	list all 'to do'	
project xyz – 2 x 1.5hr	3		
		total	10.5
Ongoing Responsibilities			
name	hours/week	name	hours/week
		total	0
interruptions, crises			0
unplanned			
others			
total needed	10.5		
total available			

Figure 6.6: Allocating time in the weekly plan

Step 2: Review your ongoing responsibilities

The first time you are doing your weekly plan, you need to list all of your ongoing responsibilities. Think about all of the ongoing meetings you have — either with other people or with yourself — on a regular basis.

Weekly List – Specific Projects			
name	hours/week	name	hours/week
hat 1 – Management		hat 3 – Sales	
induction Sue	2	proposal for AAA	1
review KPI	1	account planning	1.5
hat 2 – Strategy		review compass plan	
prepare offsite	2	list all 'to do'	
project xyz – 2 x 1.5 hr	3		
		total	10.5
Ongoing Responsibilities			
name	hours/week	name	hours/week
meeting with Manager – 30 min	0.5	client visits – 1 day per week	10
meet with direct reports – 4 x 30 min	2		
prepare team meeting – 30 min	0.5		
weekly team meeting – 1 hr	1	**Me time**	
		gym – twice a week	2
phone calls – 30 min per day	2.5	lunch – 30 min per day	2.5
emails – 1 hr per day	5	pick up kids – Wed leave office 4.30pm	
		total	26
interruptions, crises			
unplanned			
others			
total needed	36.5		
total available			

Figure 6.7: Include ongoing responsibilities in the weekly plan

On a weekly basis review your ongoing responsibilities and check the time allocated for each for next week. There should only be small modifications.

For example if you have a one-on-one with your manager, but he is away next week, put zero in front of the time needed for this activity. Or you might have four one-on-one meetings of 30 minutes each with your direct reports every week, but next week one of them is on leave. You only need 3 x 0.5 hours next week. Or Friday next week is a public holiday and therefore you only need 4 x 1 hour for emails and 4 x 0.5 hours for calls.

Weekly List – Specific Projects			
name	hours/week	name	hours/week
hat 1 – Management		**hat 3 – Sales**	
induction Sue	2	proposal for AAA	1
review KPI	1	account planning	1.5
hat 2 – Strategy		review Compass Plan	
prepare offsite	2	list all 'to do'	
project xyz – 2 x 1.5 hr	3		
		total	10.5
Ongoing Responsibilities			
name	hours/week	name	hours/week
meeting with Manager – 30 min	0	client visits – 1 day per week	10
meet with direct reports – 4 x 30 min	▪ 1.5		
prepare team meeting – 30 min	▲ 0.5		
weekly team meeting – 1 hr	1	**Me time**	
		gym – twice a week	2
phone calls – 30 min per day	● 2.5	lunch – 30 min per day	● 2
emails – 1 hr per day	● 4	pick up kids – Wed leave office 4.30pm	
		total	23.5
interruptions, crises			
unplanned			
others			
total needed	34		
total available			

▪ as manager is away   ▲ as one direct reports on leave   ● as only work 4 days

Figure 6.8: Reviewing ongoing responsibilities in the weekly plan

Review your ongoing responsibilities in light of next week. Then calculate your total for ongoing responsibilities.

Step 3: review 'me time'

Review the time committed for you, for your 'me time'. This should remain the same every week.

Then calculate your total for 'me time'.

Step 4: review the unplanned time

Again this should be the same per day in the office. Depending on the number of days in the office, calculate the total for unplanned time. If you need two and a half hours per day of unplanned time and are working four days next week, your total will be 4 x 2.5 = 10 hours.

Step 5: review and add the 'others'

Open your calendar and check all the others — all the meetings you will attend next week which have not being taken into account in the previous steps.

Simply add the number of hours needed for this.

Weekly List – Specific Projects				
name	hours/week		name	hours/week
hat 1 – Management			**hat 3 – Sales**	
induction Sue	2		proposal for AAA	1
review KPI	1		account planning	1.5
hat 2 – Strategy			review Compass Plan	
prepare offsite	2		list all 'to do'	
project xyz – 2 x 1.5 hr	3			
			total	10.5
Ongoing Responsibilities				
name	hours/week		name	hours/week
meeting with Manager – 30 min	■ 0		client visits – 1 day per week	10
meet with direct reports – 4 x 30 min	▲1.5			
prepare team meeting – 30 min	0.5			
weekly team meeting – 1 hr	1		**Me time**	
			gym – twice a week	2
phone calls – 30 min per day	●2.5		lunch – 30 min per day	● 2
emails – 1 hr per day	● 4		pick up kids – Wed leave office 4.30pm	
			total	23.5
interruptions, crises	2.5 hr per day			0
unplanned				
others	training 5 hr + supplier meet 1 hr + lunch Tony 1 hr + marketing committee 2 hr + induction Sue 2 hr			11
total needed	55			
total available				

■ as manager is away   ▲ as one direct reports on leave   ● as only work 4 days

Figure 6.9: Calculating time required in the weekly plan

Step 6: calculate and make tough effective decisions

Once all is done, you can calculate how many hours you need and how many hours you have available.

For the number of hours needed, simply add all the total calculated so far and write that figure next to 'total needed'. For the number of hours available, calculate the number of hours you will be working next week, depending on what time you get to the office and what time you leave. Write it down in 'total available' and compare to the number of hours available and the number of hours needed. Don't be surprised if the two numbers do not match; it rarely does.

It's now decision time. Differentiate between what you really need to focus on, what you can delegate, what you will not do and what you must do. This is a time where you need to think proactively; you need to think high impact rather than deadlines. And this is not easy.

When you are prioritising what you will do and will not do, take into account the long-term impact on your performance and the performance of your business of each task.

This might take a while but until the two figures match, until the number of hours needed and the number of hours available are equal, you need to continue making decisions. Do not eliminate your big rocks or increase your working hours.

By the way, you are not allowed to reduce unplanned time. This would be too easy and completely unrealistic.

Step 7: move each item in your calendar

You're nearly there. After much thinking, sweating and making tough decisions, the number of hours needed is the same than the number of hours available. Congratulations — you are ready to organise your calendar. All of your ongoing activities, along with those that don't fall into your regular routine, will already be in your calendar. Now you need to plan when you will do all the rest, all the proactive time/big rocks/specific projects.

So open your calendar and organise your time. I suggest not labelling any meeting with a general subject such as 'big rocks' or 'me time'. Be specific — write exactly the task or project you will perform during that time.

Remember to leave gaps in between all your meetings, to leave space for the 'let me breathe' time. This should not be a problem if you have allocated enough time for unplanned events.

Also take into consideration your biorhythm — when you will be the most productive for your 'thinking' time, when is best for your calls and so on. If you are a morning person, scheduling your big rocks at the end of the day might not be the best idea.

Planning weekly works

This is a very important process. This habit alone can dramatically improve your effectiveness, your focus on your big rocks. I remember one senior executive who started to do this for a few weeks. He was getting more done in less time and was feeling in control. Then he left for two weeks on leave. When he came back, he had so many things to catch up on that he did not do his weekly plan. He 'did not have the time' to do it.

The following week was an absolute nightmare for him. He was running from one crisis to another one, unprepared and ineffective. At the end of the week he felt he had achieved nothing important, he had spend no time on his big rocks, he had worked long hours and was completely stressed. 'Never again!' was his feedback to me. Since that week he has not failed once to do his weekly plan.

Remember the saying: 'By failing to plan you are planning to fail.' This is so true.

7

" I remember the first time I put an appointment in my diary to drop my daughter at school. It felt strange, as though I wasn't making most use of my time. I soon realised it's quite the opposite. I'm now managing my time to make sure I do the things that matter.

General Manager, Retail Centre of Excellence
St George Bank

Chapter 7

ACT DAILY:
TAKE ACTION REGARDLESS

Don't plan daily

Several time management companies suggest that each morning you think of what you should be doing and then schedule your day. Although this is better that not planning at all, I believe it will push you too much into being reactive, into focusing on what is urgent rather than important.

Once a quarter, do your compass plan to decide what you should focus on, and plan weekly. On a weekly basis review your compass plan, decide what you should be focusing on during the week and organise your calendar.

Then on a daily basis, the only thing you should do is check your calendar and act accordingly. Do not think on a daily basis about what you should be doing; simply act on what you have planned.

Don't try to be popular

It seems simple, but it requires a lot of discipline. You will have to fight daily to protect the time allocated for your high-impact activities. You will have blocked time on a weekly basis to work on your own on long-term, high performance projects. Every day you will be tempted to do something more urgent. Resist the temptation. This is what I call true personal leadership.

Remember the first leadership lesson from Colin Powell:

> *'Being responsible sometimes means pissing people off.*
> *Good leadership involves responsibility ... which means that*

some people will get angry at your actions and decisions. Trying to get everyone to like you is a sign of mediocrity.'

It might be a harsh thing to say, but I completely agree with Powell on this point. Saying 'yes' to everyone and jumping on all the urgent issues is a sign of mediocrity. If you want to perform, you need to be a true leader; you need to lead yourself to success regardless of the rest.

Be focused

We discussed in part two a big time waster that I call 'lack of focus'. Interruptions and distractions will not only reduce your productivity and concentration. They will also steal some precious time you should spend on your high-impact activities.

You need to be very protective of the time you have set aside to work on a high-impact activity. Often when someone calls me to organise a meeting, if they want to meet during a time I have blocked with myself to work on a high-impact activity, I apologise and mention I already have a meeting at that time. They don't have to know it is a meeting with myself.

I'll raise it again, because many of us need it 'drummed in': why do we have less respect for meeting with ourselves than with someone else? As I pointed out earlier, if you have a meeting with a very important client, it's likely you will arrive on time to the meeting. You would not dream of making a few phone calls, allowing interruptions to answer questions from colleagues, or checking your emails during the meeting. So why would you want this to happen to yourself?

I cannot emphasise this too strongly: if you have blocked some time to work on a high-impact activity, you should treat this meeting as if it were a meeting with a very important client. Start on time. Avoid interruptions. Be 100% focused on what you planned to do.

Be present

I heard recently that the average attention span is between ten and forty seconds. No, that's not ten to forty minutes. It is ten to forty seconds. We are living in a society where multi-tasking, interruptions and distractions are the norm.

We spoke at length about the danger of leaving your inbox open permanently, and to constantly jump on your computer to respond to emails, check messages or go into facebook or twitter.

One of the characteristic of high performers is their ability to be 100% present in what they are doing. They have an ability to disconnect from the rest and be 100% focused on the task at hand. One of our coaches once worked in a global accounting and consulting firm, coaching and training the firm's staff. At least once a year the global CEO would come to one of her sessions for a whole day. During that day he was there on time, did not leave regularly to check emails or messages, and stayed until the end.

She asked him how he was able to do this. She never forgot his answer: 'Christine, when I am with you in your seminar, you are the most important person for me. The rest is less important. I wouldn't be able to manage this global company effectively if I was not 100% present in all I was doing.'

Once you have decided what you will focus on — once you have done your weekly plan — act daily. Take action regardless of other factors. Be 100% present in what you are doing. This is a key point of success.

This is also true, in my view, in our private life. Be present and 100% there when you are with the people who mean the most to you. If you have a partner and children, when you come home, be 100% present with them. Don't let the stress of your working day impact the quality of your relationship with your loved ones.

Both with people and with activities you have planned in your calendar, when it is time to do them or be with them, give undivided attention. Be 100% present.

8

❝ I feel more relaxed and as such am able to think more clearly, be more creative and not just 'react' because I am running to the urgent.

Head of Practice Development
Securitor Financial Group

Chapter 8

REVIEW AND CHANGE IF NECESSARY

As mentioned, high performers are very clear on what they want to achieve, on their goals and dreams. And they are very good at regularly reviewing the best ways to perform, the best 'high-impact activities' to lead them to their goals.

As Thomas Edison wrote, 'Genius is one per cent inspiration and ninety-nine per cent perspiration.' High performers know that success is rarely a straight line. They review regularly what they want to achieve and what needs to be done to get there.

The method is quite simple. Once a year, review your goals and what you want to achieve. They are many coaches and books to guide you in writing and reviewing your long-term goals. Your long-term goals are unlikely to change dramatically every year, but some minor changes may occur.

Then every quarter, decide how to get there. Decide which high-impact activities you need to focus on. Write your compass plan.

Then once a week, do you weekly planning.

It is nothing more difficult than this. While the steps are easy, you will require some discipline. Make sure you block the time quarterly, on your own or with your team, to build your new compass plans.

Putting personal leadership into practice

Obviously there are many things to learn and digest in this section. It is absolutely worth investing time and effort to practise these principles.

Although it is important to be efficient, it is vital to be effective.

In other terms, I'd rather have someone inefficient but very effective in my team, i.e. someone messy and disorganised but aware of his/her big rocks and focusing on them, than someone very efficient but not effective, i.e. someone very well organised with clean desk, email under control and delivering on time, but spending no time on the few things which are key for his or her performance and the performance of the business.

What are you going to do differently from now on? What are you going to change?

Remember, reading is easy, changing habits is hard. You are obviously keen to learn and improve, and this is great. You have the motivation to change things. The rest should not be too difficult if you decide to practise.

Whatever you decide to take on from this chapter, practise as of today. Take thirty minutes this week, ideally today, to do the first draft of your compass plan. Take one key project and try to plan it as described in this chapter. Take a piece of paper today and draft your effective week. At the end of this week, practise your first weekly plan.

The first time you do one of the above, it will be difficult. The second time it will be a bit easier, and in a month this will have become a new habit. Be aware that practising a new habit feels weird and uncomfortable at the beginning. This is completely normal. Persist for the next three weeks.

Our work environment pushes us to be reactive — to react to all the requests, crises, emails, interruptions we face every day. As open-plan designs and hot-desks become more popular in work environments, interruptions and distractions are seen as normal. Not too long ago we were using mail to send information. By the time the letter reached the other person and they responded, a few days had gone by — sometimes a few weeks. We moved to fax for some documents, and suddenly everything went more quickly. Now most people send documents and information via email and expect an instant response. Have you ever received a call from someone asking for an answer on an email they sent fifteen minutes beforehand?

Most people are now connected to emails 24 hours a day via internet connection in their office or via their mobile phone. The speed of communication has dramatically increased, but not our capacity to think. We still need to take the time to review all these documents, to think about what each contains and then make decisions. Although we are receiving many more documents and things to do than twenty years ago, I don't think our brain and ability to think has evolved at anywhere near the same rate.

Qantas has been exploring the possibility of allowing mobile phones during flights. Apparently they have had the technology to do this for a while. When this first filtered down to the public, Qantas and its CEO received many letters from frequent flyers protesting against this idea. The one last place where they could relax and think, away from phone calls and emails, was while flying. They wanted to keep it this way.

As technological gadgets have become more accessible, and as expectations rise that we should always be 'available' via the internet, we are spending more and more time reacting, and less and less time being proactive. I believe that true success, both at a business and a personal level, is linked to being proactive. We are far more likely to be successful when we spend time on our big rocks, and focus on the few things that are key for us. It really is a constant fight to avoid being mainly caught up with reactive activities. But the choice is yours.

Every quarter when it's time to do your compass plan and plan your key projects, every week when it's time to do your weekly plan, every day when you need to act on your big rocks, the choice is yours. Do you want to be a reactive follower or a proactive leader?

Effectiveness versus happiness

In my view there is a very strong parallel between effectiveness and happiness. Being effective means being very clear about your goals and about those activities which will have a real impact in the long term on what you want to achieve, and making them a must, and then taking massive actions regardless. Well, I believe happiness is very similar.

Happiness is something everyone understands but is hard to define. How do you measure the happiness of one person versus another one? I don't think happiness is linked to the amount of money you have. I firmly believe that happiness is progress. Happiness is linked to being clear on your goals, what you want to achieve in life, and moving towards achieving them. Happiness is knowing that you are progressing towards your dreams and goals.

In business, how satisfying it is to set challenging goals, to work hard as a team towards them and to achieve them.

In personal life how amazing it is to set long-term life goals, to put effort, ingenuity and energy towards them, and to reach them.

The last word

Another few good ideas ...

All through this book you have heard me banging on the importance of practice, of habits. Edison wrote: 'Vision without execution is hallucination.' Well, for me, knowledge without practice and use is a waste of time.

Often we are contacted by organisations whose executives have heard about our approach in the area of efficiency and effectiveness and are keen to use our services. However, they are after a quick fix, a one-day session in front of 20 people to give them some good principles.

And they are always surprised when we say, 'No, this is not what we do. It's not that we don't know how to do it. Doing a one-day program on efficiency and effectiveness is no problem. It's just we don't believe in it.'

Too often people go through great 'training' programs or seminars, they hear a lot of good ideas; the next day they are back at their desk and ... nothing changes. They were sent fifty emails while away on the course, received ten voice mails and are late for several tasks. No time to practise or even think about the learning — it's straight into their old habits.

Knowledge is one thing, habits a different one.

Reading is easy; changing is hard

As you have probably found out in reading this book, the principles of efficiency and effectiveness are relatively easy. Principles such as keeping what you use daily within hand's reach, a place for everything and everything in its place, do it now/decide it now, capture and write down your ideas and thoughts, use your calendar as a reflection of your time, be clear on the two or three things which are key to your performance, put your big rocks first ... are very simple. However, transforming these principles into habits is hard.

I am sure there are a lot of things you were already doing well and that you don't need to change. But there might be a few things you can improve. Understanding the new principles is one thing; changing them into new habits is another one. You are fighting against years and years of doing the same things the same way.

Remember when I mentioned at the beginning of this book that it takes twenty-one days to change a habit? For the first few days, challenging your work habits will seem weird and will feel uncomfortable.

Whatever you want to take away from this reading, practise straight away and be persistent. It takes 21 days to change a habit. So practise and persist for 21 days, and in 21 days what you are practising will become a new habit.

Can you change with a book?

It took me several years to start writing this book. Not because I was procrastinating, but because I doubted that a book would make a difference. But, encouraged by clients and colleagues, I changed my mind. Putting the principles of effectiveness into a book might just allow more people to access these key steps and see their lives changed. I hope a book can make a difference.

My main focus is to coach people one-on-one. I am neither a writer nor a speaker. In fact writing has always been my weakness. In school and university I was always better face-to-face than in writing.

As a coach, I believe in making people practise. At first I really doubted I could have an impact on someone if I was not there to help them to practise and push them to persist.

A few years ago one of my clients asked me to work with a very large group of financial planners around the country. Because of the number of people, it was neither possibly physically nor financially to have me and my coaches to go to each of their desks to coach them. I was sceptical at first, but accepted the challenge to design a solution which would have an impact.

We decided to split the planners into groups of about ten people, and delivered three workshops for each group with three weeks between workshops. At the end of each workshop we agreed very clearly what each person needed to practise, and we asked each person to come back with evidence of the changes they had made such as photos of their desk, the number of emails in their inbox and a print-out of their calendars. We also worked very closely with the relationship managers of this bank to become our support team, to go and visit planners between sessions to help them.

The result blew me away. We received so many amazing responses at the end of this journey from planners who recognised that their new habits had transformed the way they were working. I will never forget the gentleman in Perth who came to see me at the end of it to say this journey had changed his life, or the lady in Brisbane who shook my hand so warmly, expressing her thanks and gratitude through this simple gesture. We received so many notes of thanks, that I was touched.

This really helped me to realise you can change through a series of workshops, even if the pressure is on each individual to go back to their desk and practise on their own.

I now believe the same thing is possible through a book and I sincerely hope I can help you to be more in control, be clearer on what will make you perform at work and be successful in achieving it.

Kaizen: think progress not perfection

Too often we procrastinate because we can't do things perfectly, or even 'good enough'. We wait for the perfect time to practise something, believing we must do it without blemish. And this time rarely comes.

I love the phrase 'think progress not perfection.' Whatever you want to take away from this book, just do it — even if it's not perfect, even if you don't do it the right way. Just make progress; think about each little improvement you can make.

In Japan they have a word for this: Kaizen. Kaizen can be translated into continuous improvement. In business, Kaizen refers to activities and ideas that continually improve all functions of a business, from manufacturing to management, and which come from all in the organisation, from the CEO to the most junior person.

One of our participants mentioned a great story to illustrate the Kaizen philosophy. His colleague was visiting a car manufacturing plant in Japan. He saw a big board on the wall with lots of writing on it. He did not speak Japanese so he asked his host what this board was about. 'This is our 1% improvement board,' replied the host.

The host explained: 'In our company we believe improvement can and should come from anyone, and on simple things. Many companies only focus on big changes. They ask the executives to come up with some dramatic changes or employ external consultants to make innovative suggestions. In our company we believe in the 1% improvement.

'Everyone can make simple suggestions to improve our business. For example recently one of the workers on the line suggested changing their safety belt. Until recently we were using safety belts with metal buckles. It meant we often had scratches on the car and we had to make finishing paint touches on many cars at the end of the line. After the worker's suggestion, we replaced the metal buckles with plastic ones. As a result we saved time and money. This is an example of a 1% improvement.'

I hope through this book you have bumped into many 1% improvement ideas. Don't wait; apply them straight away even if they are little and even if you will not apply them perfectly. Think Kaizen — think progress not perfection.

Let me know

I mentioned at the beginning of this book that I love receiving feedback from the people I have worked with. I mean it! Hearing the results that our approach has had in peoples' lives drives me to continue to refine and deliver our coaching. I would love to hear what you have learnt and implemented, and the impact it had for you.

Quality is a permanent quest and I want to constantly improve our approach. Therefore I place great value on your comments and suggestions. This is very important for me in order to continuously improve and provide the best.

Please do not hesitate to send me an email at cyril@wslb.com.au

Thank you for reading this book. I hope it's been a valuable use of your time.

Endnotes

Introduction

I mention research done by Lotus Development Corporation. The findings are available at http://dis.shef.ac.uk/stevewhittaker/emlch96.pdf, viewed 6 August 2010.

Regarding the 2006 study done by the University of California, Irvine researchers observed white collar workers for three days and discovered the enormous number of interruptions faced by office staff on a daily basis.

The BASEX material comes from *The Cost of Not Paying Attention: How Interruptions Impact Knowledge Worker Productivity* by Jonathan B Spira and Joshua B Feintuch in September 2005, © 2005 Basex, Inc. The PDF report can be found at http://www.basex.com/web/tbghome.nsf/23e5e39 594c064ee852564ae004fa010/ea4eae828bd411be8525742f0006cde3/$ FILE/CostOfNotPayingAttention.BasexReport.pdf

Then for my 'favourite' findings on marijuana — the research was completed for Hewlett Packard and became the subject of a BBC news article. The full story can be found by visiting http://news.bbc.co.uk/2/hi/ uk_news/4471607.stm. I do suggest you don't try this at home.

When referring to 66% of corporate strategy never being executed, my source is an article which appeared in *The Age* on 21 January 2005, titled 'Execute your strategy'.

Dr William Glasser's theories can be further explored at www.choicetheory. com, dedicated to the William Glasser Institute's mission to teach the world Choice Theory Psychology. The findings I have quoted are from Dr Glasser's book *Choice Theory* © 1998 by William Glasser and published by HarperCollins.

Chapter 1

The source material regarding how long we spend looking for things at work was cited in the business magazine *Fast Company* on 8 April 2004 using findings from a survey of 2,600 executives by Esselte, maker of Pendaflex and Dymo. Visit www.fastcompany.com

The story of Semco's new efficiency (in the section titled 'An efficient desk') can be read in more detail in *Maverick! The success story behind the world's most unusual workplace*, by Ricardo Semler. © 1993 by Tableturn, Inc., published in 1999 by Random House Business Books.

Chapter 2

Under 'Avoid time waster three: ineffective meetings', I note that up to 50% of meeting time is wasted time. This figure was qualified by Fast Meeting Co. in their article *Understanding the ROI of your Meetings*, located at http://www.fastmeetings.com.au/articles/meeting-roi-overview.htm

Chapter 3

In the section 'Efficient use of Outlook Calendar' we discussed cycles that take place throughout each night and day, and noted research by *Fast Company* magazine. The findings quoted are taken from *The Power of Full Engagement: Managing Energy, not Time is the key to High Performance and Personal Renewal* © 2003 by Jim Loehr and Tony Schwartz, published in Australia in 2003 by Allen & Unwin.

Chapter 4

In the section titled 'Think quarterly: be clear on your goals and high-impact activities', I quote from the Napoleon Hill's classic *Think and Grow Rich*. While a number of publishers have printed this book, my copy was published in the United Kingdom in 2004 by Vermillion.

Under 'Review and change if necessary', Thomas Edison's success, after failing 10,000 times to invent the light bulb, is widely quoted in print and on the web. One version can be found at http://www.thomasedison.com/quotes.html.

Chapter 5

Stephen Covey's *First Things First* was first published in Great Britain by Simon & Schuster UK Ltd, 1994 © Stephen R Covey, A Roger Merrill and Rebecca R Merrill, 1994.

I refer to General Eisenhower's emphasis on important over urgent in the section subtitled 'From reactive manager to proactive leader'. Eisenhower's priorities are accepted as a fundamental principle of effectiveness, with leading speakers and authors continuing to use the 'Eisenhower matrix'.

In the section titled 'The power of no', the quotes from Steve Jobs can be found in Leander Kahney's book, *Inside Steve's Brain* © Leander Kahney 2008, published by the Penguin Group, as can the comment from John Scully regarding what makes Steve's methodology different.

Under 'The high performance question' I encourage you to 'think Pareto'. Vilfredo Pareto (1848-1923) made significant observations regarding concentration, inequality and inverse proportion regarding Italy's wealth. You can visit http://www.csun.edu/~jmotil/Pareto.pdf (viewed 8 August 2010) for further reading.

Colin Powell's lessons can be found in *The Leadership Secrets of Colin Powell*, © 2002 by Oren Harari and published by McGraw-Hill.

Anthony Robbins' notes the findings of the Harvard Study I refer to in the section titled 'The compass plan'. His description can be found in *Unlimited Power: The New Science of Personal Achievement*, © 1996, Robbins Research Institute, published by Free Press, a division of Simon & Schuster, Inc.

I note the importance of aligning your high-impact activities to the team goals. If you'd like to peruse worthwhile books on the effectiveness of team members, try either *Time Management for Teams*, © 1992 Merrill E Douglass, published by Amacom; *Overcoming the Five Dysfunctions of a Team: A Field Guide for Leaders, Managers and Facilitators*, © 2005 by Patrick Lencioni, published by Jossey-Bass, a Wiley Imprint; and *6 Habits of Highly Effective Teams*, © 2007 by Stephen E Kohn and Vincent D O'Connell, printed in the US by Book-mart Press.

Under 'The project plan' I refer to the research of Edward Lorenz. In 1972 Lorenz presented a paper titled 'Predictability: Does the Flap of a Butterfly's Wings in Brazil Set off a Tornado in Texas?' which generated a flurry of new ideas across the scientific world. A news article that appeared after Lorenz's death in 2008 and which outlines Lorenz's contributions can be found at http://web.mit.edu/newsoffice/2008/obit-lorenz-0416.html.

Following 'the butterfly effect' I introduce the work of Edwards Deming. His impact upon Japanese manufacturing and business is legendary, and if you would like to investigate his legacy you can read a number of papers at http://www.oppapers.com/subjects/w-edwards-deming-page1.html and particularly Deming's 'Total Quality Management' principles at http://www.oppapers.com/essays/Total-Quality-Management/29673.

The extraordinarily successful *The 7 Habits of Highly Effective People* is Copyright ©1989, 2004 by Stephen R Covey and published by Free Press, a division of Simon & Schuster, Inc.

German philosopher Friedrich Nietzsche (1844-1900) is often cited in varied translations. One version of the quote I have used can be found at http://www.famousquotesandauthors.com/authors/friedrich_nietzsche_quotes.html.

Chapter 6

For details of Jim Loehr's study of sports people and their performance, read *The Power of Full Engagement: Managing Energy, not Time is the key to High Performance and Personal Renewal*, © 2003 by Jim Loehr and Tony Schwartz, published in Australia in 2003 by Allen & Unwin.

How to think like Leonardo da Vinci is a worthwhile read. Author Michael J Gelb is founder of High Performance Learning and consults for companies including AT&T and National Public Radio. *How to think like Leonardo Da Vinci* was published in 2009 by HarperElement.

The studies I refer to in 'Be in control — plan weekly religiously' come from my well-worn copy of *The Power of Full Engagement: Managing Energy, not Time is the key to High Performance and Personal Renewal*, © 2003 by Jim Loehr and Tony Schwartz, published in Australia in 2003 by Allen & Unwin.

Chapter 7

Under 'Act daily – take action regardless' I refer again to *The Leadership Secrets of Colin Powell*, © 2002 by Oren Harari and published by McGraw-Hil.

In the section titled 'Be present', I speak of the average attention span being between ten and forty seconds. This was asserted during a speech given by Doctor Adam Fraser in February 2010 on the Gold Coast during Westpac's top planner convention. Visit www.dradamfraser.com for further details.

Chapter 8

Thomas Edison's comment regarding genius, recorded under 'Review and change if necessary', was spoken in 1903 and published in *Harper's Monthly* in September 1932.

The story about executives rebelling against Qantas' ideas to allow mobile phone calls to be made in-flight is one I've heard in my years of working alongside corporations, but the source eludes me. Still, the consensus seems to be that being out of contact while flying is a nice touch in a technology-packed world.

The last word

'Vision without execution is hallucination' is attributed to Thomas Edison. Quoted generously, you can Google it as a general search or with either .edu or .gov as a prefix and you'll find plenty of examples. So I'll take this opportunity to reinforce the idea — knowledge without practice and use is a waste of time.

About the author: Cyril Peupion

A passionate coach and speaker, Cyril Peupion was born in Paris. He studied in France and worked in Europe until the age of 33. In 2001 he moved to Sydney where he lives with his wife Toni Kim, their two daughters Fleur and Mirabelle, and their son Cameron. Cyril often says that Paris is the most beautiful city in the world and Sydney the best city to live in.

Cyril initially trained as an engineer, majoring in Aeronautical and Mechanical Engineering. He soon realised he was not cut out to be an engineer and decided to do a master of Science in Management at Hautes Etudes Commerciales (HEC), the leading European business school. In Europe he worked for British Airways as Director of Sales Northern France and as General Manager of the French subsidiary of EF Corporate, world leader in language training.

In 1999, Cyril and his wife travelled around the world for six months. Newly-married, they decided to have a break from corporate life before kids. They always enjoyed travelling and had already done some great trips such as crossing part of the Sahara desert on a four wheel drive or trekking in the Andes. After a further six months touring the south island of New Zealand on a bike (2,500 km) and diving some remote and amazing places in the Pacific, Cyril and Toni Kim came to Australia and loved it. They applied for permanent residency and, in June 2001, started a new life in Sydney.

Cyril worked for several years for different companies and in 2006 launched his own business in efficiency and performance.

Cyril's business was built on both a frustration and a belief. As a fresh graduate, Cyril worked a few months for a strategic consulting firm. Although interesting, he found it frustrating to see so many great strategic ideas never executed. Companies spend a lot of effort and resources in developing their strategies. Either they hire external consulting firms, or their leadership teams undertake a number of in-depth offsite meetings throughout the year to produce their strategy. Amazingly, many of the resulting decisions are never realised. The issue is often not on the quality of the strategy and action plan decided on; it is how well these plans are turned into actions by everyone in the organisation.

Cyril's belief is that by challenging people's work habits, by challenging what they are doing on a day-to-day basis, they can significantly re-align what they are doing with what they should be doing. They can have a significant impact on their performance and that of their business. What becomes quickly apparent is that challenging and improving people's work habits has a huge impact on job satisfaction and work-life balance.

Today Cyril is the managing director of Work Smarter: Live Better. But above all, he is a passionate coach who focuses on helping people change work habits, take ownership and dramatically improve their performance.

Cyril has a solid and broad understanding of working with executives, their teams and their companies on talent development and effectiveness. He has worked closely with many senior managers and their teams in all types of industries and in different countries. His ambition is to change the lives of the people he interacts with. It may sound like a very ambitious goal, but this is what ultimately drives him.

Comments such as, 'You have changed my life,' or 'I feel so much more in control and happy with my job,' or 'My performance has dramatically increased since I have worked with you,' are the best rewards for a passionate coach.

As someone so rightly said, 'I don't care what you know until I know that you care.' Cyril's passion is to help people and, as such, participants feel it and are then open to be challenged by new ideas and to change some of their work habits.

Email: cyril@wslb.com.au
www.wslb.com.au

Speaking, Coaching, Training

Work Smarter: Live Better has one simple, clear focus: above target and in control. In other words, our aim is to transform team performance and people's lives by changing work habits.

We offer solutions that include executive coaching and mentoring for senior leaders, group coaching for management groups, training for large groups, workshops and keynote speeches, all the way to the book *Work Smarter: Live Better*, a bestseller in the top 10 business books in Australia.

Feedback from our clients speaks better than lengthy explanation:

Praise for our coaching and training solutions

'It is hard to precisely quantify the improvement on the performance of the team (of 6 people). However I estimate we saved between half a million to a million dollars of cost thanks to this journey. The increased focus of the team probably accelerated some key projects by about 6 months.'

'I would recommend that anyone who is looking to achieve more in their day with less stress and greater sense of control should participate in this course. It will change your life!'

'We've increased our client facing time by 28%. As a result the size of our pipeline has doubled, and our Net Promoter Score moved from 64% to 84%.'

'A very big Thank You for sharing and promoting such an amazing journey!'

'On the back of completing the Efficiency Workshop with no word of a lie, my life has changed! Not only professionally, but personally as well. I have never felt so consistently calm in a work environment ever, and I often find myself "preaching" the benefits of this journey to my peers.'

'I think the program is outstanding. If only every organization adopted these practices, the country would be a lot more efficient.'

Praise from our keynote speeches

'One of the best presentations I have ever seen!'

'Outstanding.'

'I will take tools away and implement – fabulous.'

'Work Smarter: Live Better was the standout session of the FPA conference receiving the most number of votes.'
FPA (Financial Planning Association) conference

'It was voted by my team "hands-down the most incredible learning session we have had." I presume that's why "life-changing" was a word that came up so often in the feedback.'
Founder & Director of a leading Australian retailer

'I can't put it into words. I have never seen a single session and presenter have such an impact! It was the core theme today and the takeaway actions flowed into the team planning session this afternoon and report back.'
CEO of one of the largest insurance groups in Australia

Praise for the book, *Work Smarter: Live Better*

'I wanted to give you some further feedback on your book after reading and implementing it. Here's what's happened in the last quarter: My sales have increased by 173% from last quarter and I actually am working less days of the week and find I have achieved more. In fact I say "no" more than I say "yes" and I manage to do more.'

'Just wanted to send you a quick email to say a big THANKS! Wow, what an impact on the running of my business and my personal life.'

'I want to thank you for the massive impact your book is having on my life! I am slowly implementing a number of your suggestions and my productivity has gone through the roof already, and I'm only half way through the book!'

'I am enjoying your book immensely, and I look forward to the new life that awaits me.'

For more information, please contact:

Work Smarter: Live Better
www.wslb.com.au
Email: contact@wslb.com.au

hard nosed

actual

log the

deeken

else.

not as

tender feel

e?>

ble

iead
ful

100 mpleuer
2nd rond fadig
Richted org
John 1st drect
hire
⟶ brought ops
asses Stak of org
pul neight not
Fuctual

large conf room
leadrship lab Stetch
balance - mothads
coach ⟶ mentory ppl
able ⟶ Sehsan
respect, dectsihes

New vision man —

artemes

Grau

menu
Offer the

press hours

John

COO
USO ——— broad band Ans ⟶ AOL

Yau uey ?s   NFP
     o forces.
                    I hu
   muler   aclude
    sunt   tc s
  ceushy Rum
      toglus i unburd

K|2 ΣГР decaoln

untom
pnuden Ercler
fmed f fexur